AF156407

Dr. Priyadarshi Bahinipati

Jagamohana Ramayana

The Epic of Balarama Dasa

Anchor Academic
Publishing

Bahinipati, Priyadarshi: Jagamohana Ramayana. The Epic of Balarama Dasa, Hamburg, Anchor Academic Publishing 2017

Buch-ISBN: 978-3-96067-124-4
PDF-eBook-ISBN: 978-3-96067-624-9
Druck/Herstellung: Anchor Academic Publishing, Hamburg, 2017
Covermotiv: © pixabay.de

Bibliografische Information der Deutschen Nationalbibliothek:
Die Deutsche Nationalbibliothek verzeichnet diese Publikation in der Deutschen Nationalbibliografie; detaillierte bibliografische Daten sind im Internet über http://dnb.d-nb.de abrufbar.

Bibliographical Information of the German National Library:
The German National Library lists this publication in the German National Bibliography. Detailed bibliographic data can be found at: http://dnb.d-nb.de

CONTENTS

PREFATORY NOTE

One of the main subsistence of the ancient Sanskrit literatures and Medieval literatures of different parts of India are Rama and Krishna oriented themes. Form Valmiki Ramayana in Sanskrit to Ramayana in different vernacular languages of Tamil, Telgu, Malayalam, Kannada, Assamese, Gujarati, Bengali, Odishi, Marathi, Hindi all have proceeded from the rudimentary stage of local language literatures to become Mahakavyas in their respective areas and reached every nook and corners of the region, galvanizing the mind and hearts of the populace. Although they have been composed in different periods and the poets and composers have a different style of presentation of their own they acquired the status of original spokesperson of Ramayana in their respective regions. It is a fact that Indian languages and literatures are enriched by the form, content, ideas and ideologies of the epics of yesteryears.

Rama after being accepted as an incarnation of Vishnu and after the popularization of devotion of Rama in the fourteenth century, all the literatures were intertwined in the current of a feeling of love and devotion. This trend has been manifested in the work of Balarama Dasa, one of the doyens of litterateurs of medieval Odisha. He equated Rama with Lord Jagannath and named his version of Ramayana as Jagamohana Ramayana itself. He belonged to a group of litterateurs who were famous in the history of Odisha as Panchasakhas and were known for their sublimity, egalitarianism and intellectualism.

For generation together Ramayana has not only remained as a part and parcel of poetry or epic rather it evolves through ages as a source of inspiration for living an ideal life. Rama and Sita has become a symbol of an epitomized idealistic character of the Indian culture, which continued to provide paths to get higher ends of life.

It is therefore essential to discuss the vernacular literatures which provided salubrity to the culture of Odisha and how they were penned with a view to enrich the valued tradition of the society as morality, ethics, healthy beliefs and practices are always ageless. It is always important to revisit the works of literatures in different periods to find out the state of mind of those writers and composers who generated their literary marvels to establish their views emphatically with a reformative approach. In Odisha, the Panchasakhas were the champions of liberty, fraternity and equality for which it is all the more important to analyse their works time and again to escalate the idea of free thought and expression and rescue the gamut of their opinions and ideas from intellectual hibernation.

Tripura — Priyadarshi Bahinipati

01.02.2017

THE PROLOGUE

Ramayana is the first great epic in Indian literature. From the point of thought, expression, metre, mode of composition, flavor of composition it acquired a sublime status in primeval literatures of the world.

It is an inherent part of life of the Indians as it is not only a repertoire of religious and moral ideals but also important from the point of humanity oriented social scripture where the inherent meaning of life can be found. It is a mirror of the heritage of India, of the thoughts, perception, hopes and aspiration of the people hitherto. Its popularity is not because of the personification of the God rather it is famous because it revolves around the characters of an ideal father, ideal son, ideal mother, ideal brother, ideal husband, ideal wife, ideal friend, ideal servant, etc.

Sage Valmiki had given utmost importance to idealism because he envisioned that morality and idealism would provide an ethical and value based society. Much importance has given to the behavioural aspects of human being, which revolves around the character, honour, reputation between relationships, and these are the essence on which a social fabric rests. The ideals and morality, which were preached and practiced during that period, are still relevant today which is evident from the popularity Ramayana enjoys even now.

It has become possible to compose Ramayana in different local and vernacular languages only after tenth century A.D. During the fifteenth to sixteenth century A.D. Balarama Dasa had composed Ramayana in Odia which became famous as Jagamohana Ramayana. Even a number of compositions have been made afterwards but its popularity has not been surpassed until today. Although, Ramayana has been written in many Indian languages, however these are not the exact translation of the Valmiki Ramayana and there are regional variations. They have their own regional specialty and contemporaniety where different socio-political religious issues of the time have been incorporated. However, the fact remains that all the Ramayana's are thematically same and there soul is one.

Jagamohana Ramayana is the first Ramayana composed in Odia language. Balarama Dasa's exposition was the reflection of the spirit of the age particularly in Odisha when the manifestation of the popular sentiment through lucid compositions was initiated by a group of illustrious personalities famous in the annals of Odishan history as the Panchasakhas of which Balarama Dasa himself was a camaraderie. They epitomized certain elements in the society in the medieval age like rationalism, reason and conscience which revolutionalised the process of thinking. They had given prominence to subaltern concepts and ideology and through their writings enriched the cultural and literary heritage of Odisha.

In ancient time, Odisha was mainly divided into three parts such as- Udra/Odra, Utkala and Kalinga. In the opinion of Cunningham the extent of these three regions were as- Udra constituted the region of west Midnapore and possibly Manbhum or east Singhbhum and south Bankura; Utkala constituted the area from the south of Kapisa river to northern part of Baitarani river and from the coastal Balasore to Lohardaga near Ranchi and Sirguja of Madhaya Pradesh; Kalinga constituted the area from the south of Baitarani river to Langulya of Visakhapatanam and from the east-coast to Amarkantak region of Madhaya Pradesh.

This extent of Odisha was continued to change over the subsequent periods. The kingdom of Utkala while extended up to the river Mahanadi, the kingdom of Kalinga was extended up to river Godavari. Therefore, in ancient time it was known that Udra constituted the northern part, Utkala, the central part and Kalinga the southern part of Odisha.

During the reign of the Suryavamsi Gajapatis the extent of Odisha was from Ganga in the north to Godavari in the south. In different periods several smaller kingdoms like Kangoda, Kosala, Trikalinga etc. rose and were dissolved with these three large constituents. There is historical evidence that during the reign of Anantavarman Chodoganga Deva of Ganga Dynasty (11th- 12th century A.D.) these three kingdoms were united to form an empire called Udra. Since then the region was known as Udra or Utkala. During the Marathas and the British the term Odisa and Orissa has been in use instead of Utkala.

Towards the end of the eleventh century A.D., there was the rule of the Gangas in Odisha who ruled until the middle of the fifteenth century A.D. There were in toto fifteen rulers who ruled for three hundred fifty seven years (1078-1435A.D.). The founder of this dynasty, Anantavarman Chodoganga Deva ruled from 1078 to 1147 A.D. united the whole of Odisha and during his reign the extent of his empire was from Ganga to Godavari which proves his prowess and strength.

By the time of the accession of the third ruler of the dynasty, Rajaraja Deva-III (1188-1211 A.D.) there occurred a big political transformation in northern India. Due to the absence of any powerful empire in India, the Muslims successfully established themselves as the rulers by defeating the disjunctive forces that were in operation in India one by one in tandem. Their victory was emphatic after the defeat of Prithiviraj Chouhan which was the *coup d' grace* that led to the beginning of a new era in the political arena. The Muslims were not content with their initial victories rather they started to consolidate and expand their empire by conquering new territories. Eventually they marched towards the east and captured Lakhnauti, the capital of Gauda. The Sena ruler Lakshman Sena fled without fighting which led to the establishment of first Muslim rule in Bengal under Ikhtiyar-ud-din Muhammad Bakhtiyar Khilji who became the first Nawab of Bengal.

Ikhtiyar Khilji was not content with his occupation of Bengal but tried to expand his empire in the east to Assam and Odisha. However, he did not get any immediate success in Odisha because of the powerful rule of the Gangas. Ikhtiyar Khilji sent his faithful commanders Muhammad-i-Seran and Ahmad-i-Seran to occupy Lakhnor and Jajnagar in 1205 A.D.

However, due to the demise of Ikhtiyar-ud-din during the exploits of Kamrup these two commanders returned to Bengal. Though it has not been mentioned, in Tabaqat-i-Nasiri that the two commanders were defeated but this has been known from other sources.

The Muslims attacked Odisha during the reign of Rajaraja Dev-III, which has been considered by many historians as the first and foremost attack of Odisha by the Muslims. From 1205A.D. to 1568 A.D., the Muslims attacked Odisha again and again but in vain and Odisha succeeded to maintain its identity as an independent Hindu kingdom. The other great kings of the Ganga dynasty like Anangabhima Deva-III (1211A.D.-1238A.D.), Narasimha Deva-I (1238A.D.-1264A.D.) and the king of Suryavamsi dynasty like Gajapati Kapilendra Deva (1435A.D.-1468A.D.), Purusottama Deva (1468A.D.-1497A.D.) not only protected Odisha from Muslim invasions but also attacked their territories time and again in order to expand their own empire.

It was during the reign of Prataparudra Deva (1497A.D.-1533A.D.) turmoil in Odisha started. During his reign, the boundary of his empire started to contract and towards the end of his reign the extent of empire remains from Ganga to Krishna river. Up to thirty-five years after the death of Prataparudra Deva, Odisha was able to maintain its independence. According to Akbarnamah after the death of the last Hindu ruler Mukunda Deva, Odisha lost its independent identity in 1568A.D. and the Muslim rule was started in Odisha.

Poet Balarama Dasa was born during the reign of Gajapati Purusottama Deva (1468A.D.-1497A.D.). Due to the peace, tranquility and prosperity in that period a lot of cultural development took place, which reached its zenith after the establishment of Suryavamsa in Odisha. As is evident from ancient times that cultural atmosphere was created on the basis of religion, in Odisha also it is found that its cultural edifice was erected on the Jagannath Dharma. The mention of Srikhetra can be found in Mahabharata (Vanaparva) from which it is established that from very early times worship of Jagannath was prevailed in Odisha. Because in different periods Odisha was the meeting ground of different religions like, Buddhism, Jainism, Shaktism, Vaishnavism, Saivism etc. there prevailed a syncretic atmosphere.

In the ninth century A.D. during the reign of Kesari dynasty, the visit of Adi Sankaracharya to Srikhetra led to the resurrection of Brahmanism in Odisha.

After the Kesaris, came the Gangas and the founder of this dynasty Chodoganga Deva though a Saivite after the conquest of Utkala became a Vaishnava follower. During his reign his contemporary the famous religious preacher Ramanujacharaya (1056-1137A.D.) visited Srikhetra and beatified and initiated him into Vaishnavism. Along with this process, Brahmanism and Vaishnavism started in Odisha. Ramanujacharya's disciple Govinda established the Emar Math in Srikhetra. After that the followers of Madhavacharya, Ramananda visited Srikhetra and established their respective *mathas* there. In the reign of the greatest rulers of the Ganga and Surya dynasty, Brahmanism and Vaishnavism had assumed the status of a royal religion and as such in the religious consciousness of Odisha, Vaishnavism and Vaishnava thoughts and sentiment had acquired a niche for itself.

By the time of composition of Balarama Dasa's Jagamohana Ramayana i.e., last decade of fifteenth century A.D., Buddhism, Jainism, Brahmanism, Nath religion, Tantric Buddhism and Vaishnavism with its branches has established themselves firmly on the soil of Odisha.

In the medieval period there emerged the famous social reform movement known as the Bhakti Movement, which was a movement of the people and was an attempt on the part of the reformers and preachers to remove the socio religious injustice that over the centuries had engendered bitter strife amongst the various folds of society and tried to impart them a better homogeneity and sense of peace and security. It was a movement against social regression and bigotry of all religions. The reformers exposed the futility of all outwardly ceremonies and emancipated the mind of the people from the domination of priests and mullahs. They minimized religious favouritism, fanaticism and intolerance, arrested the growth of irrational life and promoted self-knowledge. The impact of this movement could also be found in Odisha.

The sixteenth century was a remarkable period in the history of Odisha. It was an era of reform and development of consciousness for social equality. There was a cultural renaissance during this period spearheaded by a group of saint poets to raise mass consciousness against the dominant and ruling elements of the time. They were famous as Panchasakhas or the five friends- Balarama Dasa, Jagannatha Dasa, Achyutananda Dasa, Yasovanta Dasa and Ananta Dasa. Four of these Panchasakhas were *sudras* (lower caste in the four fold social structure) except Jagannatha Dasa who was a Brahmin. They protested against caste, untouchability, discrimination of women and the Brahmin monopoly of knowledge. All of them renounced their caste or original surnames and adopted the surname "Dasa" (servant of God) as mark of protest against the caste. The main objective of their movement was the establishment of a society based on equality and justice. Their teachings were in conformity with medieval *Bhakti* ideals such as:

"Jat panthe puche na koi
Hariko bhaje so Harika hoi"

i.e. Who asks of caste and birth of the people who worship Hari and belong to him.

The writings and preaching of Panchasakhas invoked the wrath of the dominant vested interest but in spite of innumerable obstacles and difficulties they endeared themselves to the common folks by their genuine emphasis on egalitarianism. They did not want to found a new religion but reform Hinduism with the objective of bringing social harmony, Universal brotherhood, social equality and stability. In Odisha, Puri was a great centre of learning and education then. The pundits and Sanskrit scholars from the nook and corner of the country congregated there to participate in intellectual discourses. Great saints of the fifteenth century

India like Ramanuja, Nanak, Tulsidas, Kabir, Chaitanya, Vallabhacharya visited Puri to spread their gospels and therefore it was regarded as the highest centre of fusion and exchange of ideas. It is noteworthy that earlier in the eighth century Sankaracharya made it one of the four pontifical seats of the Hindus situated in the four corners of India. Therefore, it is quite natural that the Panchasakhas in their lifetime had chosen and associated with this place to establish their credentials.

Despite being the establishment of a number of religious sects in Odisha, the Panchasakhas had never accepted or followed any particular religion, faith or sect rather they respected all the prevalent ideologies sans their rigidity and followed their own principles and ideology guided by sufficient amount of ratiocination.

There are differences of opinion, as there is no established proof about the date and time of Balarama Dasa and his Jagamohana Ramayana. Thus, all that is said and written about him is based on indirect and circumstantial evidences. Scholars have opined differently regarding his birth some of which are:

Nilamani Mishra-1460A.D.; Pt. Mrutunjay Tripathy-1470A.D.; Dr. Ramanath Tripathy-1470-80A.D.; Dr. Artaballav Mohanty-1472A.D.; Pt. Suryanarayan Dash-1473A.D.; Dr. Mayadhar Manasingh-1482A.D.; Surendra Mohanty-1484A.D.

The Panchasakha period has been ascribed by many as the age of translation as a number of famous Sanskrit scriptures were translated into Odia. The literatures composed in those days were meant for the understanding of common people and therefore vernacular language was used and difficult themes were very lucidly explained. Those compositions were regularly read and recited in the *'bhagavata tungis'* and temples so that people belonging to all the sections of the society could listen to them which helped them to build their character based on morality and ethics.

By the fifteenth century, there emerged a sort of awakening in the society for the translation of Sanskrit *shastras* in vernacular and local languages. Throughout India, there was an effort in this regard so that people can accept and understand the course and inherent meaning of the vast repository of Sanskrit literatures in their own language.

Following this trend Sarala Dasa had already written the Mahabharata much before sixteenth century A.D. Towards the end of fifteenth century A.D. and in the beginning of sixteenth century A.D. i.e. the transitional period, Balarama Dasa had become renowned by writing his Jagamohana Ramayana. He also tried to unfetter the popular religious texts from the iron chain of Sanskrit. Due to this attempt of Balarama Dasa, he had undergone the reproach and derision at the hands of the holder of religious flag and the social pundits of the time. In face of such criticism and opposition, he daringly established the rights of all and sundry in the society to participate and discuss the *shastras* and *puranas*. Because of his daring initiative, the Odia literature was enriched by the rich colloquial exposition of Jagamohana Ramayana which found a place in the heart and soul of the Odias.

If the religious history of India and history of the various concepts of history are to be considered it can be found that, some factual details about the concept and ideal of religious practices can be found during the Vedic period. In the four Vedas there are several contents in the form of hymns, which reveals the various forces of gods and goddesses. However, it is quite pertinent to think that before the Vedic Aryans the whole of the then India was inhabited by non-Aryans who were termed differently as Dravidians, Nishads, Kirat in Sanskrit language. The discovery of Indus Valley Civilisation is a proof, which brought to fore the existence of indigenous civilization and culture in India. They have their own form of socio-religious, political system which is reflected in the artifacts and archaeological remains found at different sites. It has been found that they unlike the Aryans were the worshippers of idols.

The Vedic Aryans worshipped different forces of nature but towards the later Vedic period, a differential approach was noticed through a number of interpretations, commentaries that were famous as Brahmanas, Aranyakas, Upanishads etc. And the sign of *bhakti* can also be found in the Vedas. It is obvious that a number of changes might have occurred among the Aryans after coming into contact with numerous indigenous cultures and faiths. The survival and continuity of Indus Valley cultures in the later periods is a fact to be reckoned with. In the Upanishads importance has been given to *jnana* and in that path of knowledge it is quite visible that there is manifestation of *karma* and *bhakti* altogether.

After this Vedic and Upanishadic period, there was the development of Puranic age where *bhakti* was given the utmost importance. This manifestation of different forms cannot be seen in isolation, as it was a gradual development of thoughts, ideas and concepts from time to time with the changing circumstances. The concept of *bhakti* has evolved through centuries particularly during the Gupta Age when the Bhagavata Dharma was widely prevalent and it received the status of sate religion. In the Pncharatra Samhita composed during this time, the bhakti concept related evidences have been traced. The Svetasvetara Upanishad, Narad Bhakti Sutra, Sandilya Bhakti Sutra, Srimad Bhagavat Gita, Srimad Bhagavat etc. are the repertoire where there are ample evidences of *bhakti* can be found. In order to know the definition, forms and types of bhakti one has to go through these texts.

The word *bhakti* comes from the Sanskrit *bhaj dhatu* whose simple meaning can be *bhajan* where a devotee sings panegyrics of a particular god or goddess to whom he/she is devoted to express their inner cravings and seek blessing in this world and hereafter. It is regarded as an act of communication with God.

Though the sign of *bhakti* could be found in the Vedic literatures, its gradual growth and development has been made with an orientation towards Vaishnava Dharma. Both Vaishnava Dharma and the concept of *bhakti* are complimentary to each other and the magnificent edifice of Vaishnava Dharma has been erected on the foundation of *bhakti*. Among the *bhakti* oriented Hindu worshipers and sects the majority belong to the Vaishnava sect and as such this sect gained popularity and eventually a number of branches of this sect were created.

The revering deity of Vashnavism is Vishnu. Then there are theories of various scholars came to fore which tried to find the provenance of Vishnu. Scholars found that the worship of Vishnu was there before the Aryans and the pre-Aryan race i.e. the Dravidians. They considered Vishnu as the snake deity. Afterwards when the Aryans came they assimilated a number of socio-cultural practices and accepted Vishnu as a God of their own. Due to the innumerable description of Vishnu in the oldest literature of India, the Rig Veda it can be unequivocally accepted that Vishnu is an ancient Vedic god.

In the post-Vedic era, Vishnu emerged not only as a famous god but also got the supreme, ultimate, infinite position. Aiterya Aranyak, Aiterya Brahman, Satapatha Brahman etc. describes the ultimate status of Vishnu. There is a unique combination of earthly and ethereal traits found in Vishnu for which he is not only considered as a god but also a Supreme Being.

Because he is adorned with many humanly attributes and because of his multifarious personality, he is considered as the protector of earth and heaven and as such, he became the foremost deity of the Vashnavites. Besides this for the assistance of other gods and human beings later, a number of incarnations have been imagined.

During the period when Mahabharata was written, the Vaishnava Dharma has taken a concrete shape in the form of Bhagavata Dharma or Satwat Dharma. But from when exactly the Bhagavata Dharma originated is shrouded in mystery, however according to many scholars it can be assumed that before fifth century B.C. it had taken a definite form.

A number of inscriptions of ancient period like – the Besanagar Pillar (Garuda) Inscription, which speaks about the acceptance of Bhagavata Dharma by Heliodorous, the ambassador of Greek king Antialkidas denote the practice and popularity of Bhagavata Cult. Another important development was the worship of Vasudeva Krishna by the followers of Satwat Dharma. From many inscriptions like Nanaghat Inscription (2nd century B.C. to 1st century A.D.), the name of Vasudeva is mentioned along with others. Thus, by taking into consideration the different sources available it can be said that from fifth century B.C. to fifth century A.D. Vasudeva Krishna became the revered deity of *bhakti*-oriented sects. Similarly, from Meghasthenes Indica, from Tolemy's account the existence of worshipers of Vasudeva in and around Mathura, in the vicinity of river Bitasta can be ascertained.

Like in the north India, in south India also there are evidences of the spread and practice of Vaishnava Dharma. From the Satavahana inscription of Gautamiputra Sri Jajnasri Satakarni it is clear that there was Bhagavata Dharma in Andhra Pradesh.

Thus, the worship of Vasudeva Krishna is amply found in Mahabharata and later on a link was established between Vishnu, Narayana, Vasudeva Krishna which is evident from the Vanaparva in Mahabharata where Krishna described himself umpteen times as Vishnu. So gradually all these names became synonymous signifying one God and with this Vaishnava Dharma developed to the fullest extent. The importance of Krishna also continued in the Puranic Age.

As in north India, in south India also the *bhakti* concept and *bhakti* oriented sects were active during the first few centuries A.D. The evidences in this regard can be found in

Silappadikaram and other Tamil literatures, which mention that in Madurai, Caveripattinam and some other places there were ancient temples where Krishna and Balaram were worshipped. As there is mention of Vishnugopa of Pallava dynasty of Kanchi in Allahbad Prasasti it can be assumed that in Gupta period in South India there was the use of the name of Vishnu. There are ample evidences recovered from the temples of Mahabalipuram and even some of the inscriptions of the Chalukya monarchs prove the existence of the concept of Vaishnavism in southern India.

In the development and spread of Vaishnava bhakti in South India the role of the Alvars cannot be undermined. They composed innumerable poems and panegyrics devoted to Vishnu. As from the first century A.D., evidences are there regarding the existence of Alvars is no gainsaying the fact that they were the early propagators of Vaishnava *bhakti* concept. This spread of the path of love and devotion in South India later in some way or other influenced the *bhakti marga* in Odisha and even Chaitanya's concept of *bhakti* in Bengal.

Another important aspect of the Alvars was that there was no discrimination on the basis of caste and creed and all from the kings to the common man belonging to the untouchables, even to the women class were accepted unhindered in to the sect. From seventh century A.D. to the tenth century A.D. for about 350 years, these Alvars took the Vaishnava concept of *bhakti* to different areas of the South India. Although during that time Vendantist like Sankaryacharya's doctrine of '*Adwaitavad*' and '*Mayavad*' had affected the concept of *bhakti* still the simplicity and lucidity in explaining their doctrine through compositions in colloquial languages attracted the people and they succeeded in retaining their base.

The rule of Sankaracharya in the revival and development of Indian Culture cannot be denied and underestimated. He belonged to a time when there was a sort of lull in the religious atmosphere of India. All the reactionary religions like the Jainism and Buddhism were in the process of decline. A number of new sects were growing like the Vajrayana, Sahajayana in Buddhism, which practiced some unconventional way of worship. During this time, the existence of Vedic Brahmanical religion also dwindled and its progress slackened in the absence of any illustrious pathfinder and intelligent expositor. At this critical juncture, the emergence of Sankaracharya was a blessing for Brahmanism. He gave new direction by his interpretation of

Upanishadic conception of religion and orgainsed the Hindu society with a renewed vigour and to an extent decimated the anti-Vedic sects that were in operation in India.

Although Sankaracharya succeeded in infusing a new life into the spiritual life of India, however it did not affect the way of worship of common people because his difficult concept of '*Adwaitavad*' was not understandable to the ordinary folks. In such a situation, it was quite natural that the people were attracted towards the *bhakti* concepts of Alvars and the Nayanars in the South India. After Sankaracharya the purpose of almost all the preceptors who established their own sects based on their own doctrines and ideologies were:

a) the establishment of Vedic religion;
b) the expulsion and rejection of anti-Vedic religions;
c) the indoctrination of the people by refuge oriented *bhakti* or devotion.

All these preachers by promenading in different parts of India tried to disseminate Vaishnavism and despite being minor differences in their own concepts of Vaishnavism they took it to the nooks and corners of India.

In the post-Sankara period, several Vaishnava saints refuted the '*Adwaitavad*' of Sankara and through their sects tried to popularise Vaishnavism. Prominent among them was 'Sri' sect of which Ranganathacharya, Ramanujacharya were important preachers who established '*Visisthadwaitavad*'. Ramananda was also belonged to this sect and it was he who established Ramayet Vaishnava sect.

Similarly, Madhavacharya established the 'Brahma' sect. He and his followers also refuted Sankara's '*Adwaitavad*' and preached pure dualism or '*visuddha dwaitavad*'.

Then another sect famous as 'Sanakadi' sect of which famous preacher Nimbarka and his followers popularised 'Radha-Krishna' worship. He preached '*dwaita-dwaitavad*'.

In the first half of the sixteenth century A.D. two most prominent Vaishnavite preachers who preached Vaishnavism and Radha-Krishna worship were Vallabhacharya of 'Rudra' cult and Sri Chaitanya of 'Gaudiya' sect or 'Madhava' sect. Vallabhacharya propagated '*Suddhadwaitavad*' in western India. Chaitanya preached '*Achintyabhedabheda*' concept.

All the Vaishnava preachers of the above-discussed sects gave prominence to *'saguna'* concept of *bhakti* refusing Sankara's *'nirguna' bhakti* and worshipped Brahma in the form of Hari, Vishnu, Narayana and Krishna.

The concept of *'Ramabhakti'* in Vaishnavism had grown particularly when Adikavi Valmiki composed Ramayana depicting the idealism and noble character of human being. He on several occasions compared Ramachandra with Vishnu in Ramayana. Much before a link and relationship was established between Lord Rama and Vishnu and in Brahmanical religion the concept of incarnation or '*avataravad'* had already been devised.

When and how the relationship of Vishnu and Rama was established can be gleaned from the fact that in second century B.C. when the Sunga dynasty was established after the decline of the Mauryas, Buddhism had already established its superiority all over and the trend of worshipping Buddha as an incarnation of God was initiated. And during this time the followers of Brahmanism in order to protect their own religion from intrusion established a relationship of Vishnu with Rama. In the Puranic Age a number of Vishnu oriented compositions were made like, Vayu Purana, Matsya Purana, Brahmanda Purana, Bhagavata Purana and Himavamsa, wherein the incarnation of Rama had been described as the seventh incarnation in line in the list of incarnations of Vishnu. Consequently, in the gradual development of '*bhaktivad'* i.e. devotionalism two main human incarnations of Rama and Krishna had already spread their influence in the life of the Indians to such an extent that the people started to give prominence to these two incarnations than Vishnu.

Like the form of worship of Krishna which was evident from the fifth century B.C. and there were the growth of sects centering around the worship of Krishna such as Bhagavata cult, no such sect or cult developed centering around the worship of Rama. The evidence of organized and sectarian way of worshipping Rama actually started in the eighth century A.D. and afterwards. In the post-Gupta era when the importance of Bhagavatism and Vaishnavism declined due to lack of royal patronage, it found an appropriate place in the current of *bhakti* in Southern India and the Alvars popularised it by laicizing it.

Down the line of sects and preachers propagating 'Ramabhakti', the most important was Ramananda who can be attributed the status of progenitor of 'Ramabhakti'. Ramananda vociferously protested against the caste discrimination and for his generosity, he was condemned and ousted from his place and out of disgust, he left Srirangam and went to north India which he accepted as his place of action. He established a new sect by rising above caste, creed and religion, which became famous as per his name Ramanandi sect. Because of his all-encompassing and inclusive attitude he accepted disciples from different section of the society disregarding caste, creed, religion some of which were Raidas, who was a Chamar, Kabir who was a Muslim and he even accepted women as his disciples. He made no distinction between the Brahmins and members of disregarded castes and all could dine together as they were devotees of Vishnu.

He used the vernacular language i.e. Hindi instead of Sanskrit to describe the views, ideas and thoughts of the sect. He disliked the narrow circumference of socio-religious privileges of the conservative and higher echelons of the society and tried to ensure freedom of religion, race, sex and caste so that the neglected, oppressed and despised would attain equality of status and opportunity as human being in the society. Such was the magnanimity of Ramananda that through his indomitable efforts the current of *bhakti* reached all and sundry.

He established centres or *mathas* at different pilgrimages in Northern and Eastern India in order to stop proselytisation. He tried to enthuse fearlessness and courage amongst his followers by prompting them to worship that form of Rama, which bears bow and arrow. Thus, the disciples of his sect tried to keep themselves healthy through physical exercises and training in the use of arms and ammunition. Therefore, later, a number of *akhadas* or gymnasiums were established. Not only had this he also tried to inculcate the spirit of an ideal human being in society by preaching the idealism, characteristic earnestness, morality of Rama and Sita. He had not isolated himself from the worldly life by becoming an ascetic rather he tried to reform the malignant society and save it from depravity and instability. He used the religious platform to unite the people and spread among them rationalism to rejuvenate their thought, expression and belief so that society can evolve from mundane and moribund state and attain happiness of the highest order which is spiritualism in real sense of the term. He never confined himself to any compartmentalised and parochial thought and accepted all the good elements of the different sects and used them to attain the ultimate truth.

In Odisha among the Panchasakhas one of the illustrious and apostolic figure was Balarama Dasa who was the eldest of them. During the time of social and cultural turmoil in the sixteenth century Odisha, Balarama Dasa emerged on the scene and through his writings tried to leverage the falling society. He respected all but, he did not have any castiest consideration and always accepted the superiority of the devotees of God. He never endured injustice without reproach. He experienced the existence of Jagannath in each and every inch of his life and thus dedicated all his works to him.

His association with Puri from childhood brought him closer to the pundits there. Almost all his literary creations were Jagannath oriented. He had written around thirty or more books. From his compositions, Jagamohana Ramayana, Brahmanda Bhugola, Vedanta Sara Gupta Gita, Bata Abakasha Bhaba Samudra, Lakshmi Purana, Kanta Koili, Baula Adhyay, Ganesh Bibhuti Tika, Saptanga Yog Saratika, Bedha Parikrama, Virat Gita, Bhagavat Gita, Jnana Chudamani etc. are important. In these writings, there is a reflection of his poesy and his disregard for the existing superstition like untouchability in the society. His eagerness and effort had always been to establish and propagate the concept of Vaishnavism of Utkala (Odisha). His motto was to revolutionise the religious beliefs through literature which is amply reflected in his Ramayana.

Before delving into the Jagamohana Ramayana it is necessary to know about Lord Jagannath to whom Balarama Dasa completely dedicated himself. Odisha is known as the abode of Lord Jagannath. The relationship of Lord Jagannath with the Odiyas is so deep and intimate that the culture of Odisha is known as Jagannath Culture and the religion as Jagannath Dharma. There are differences of opinions regard the origin of Jagannath Dharma. Many considered that Brahmanism, many Jainism and Buddhism and still others considered tribal religion played an important part in its growth and development. In the opinion of Brahmin protagonists, he is Vedic deity Purusottama, for the votaries of Buddhism he is a Buddhist, in the view of Jainas he is Risabhanath and for the Saivites he is Lord Siva. But, Jagannath has not been the revered deity of any particular group or sect. Rather he was established as a unified whole and the Jagannath Dharma in due process of time became a symbol of divine syncretism. Its universality has been proved and strengthened time and again with the visit of practitioners, preachers, propagators of a number of sects and faiths from all over the country to Puri which is also famous as Srikhetra.

Therefore, it is a place where conglomeration of all the ideas, ideologies and faiths occurred and all of them metamorphosed into Jagannath Dharma.

By the eighth century A.D., Ramayana had become popular in Odisha as is evident from a number of compositions of that period. Sarala Dasa had also mentioned in brief about Ramayana in his magnum opus, Mahabharata. But it was Jagamohana Ramayana of Odisha where Ramabhakti has been amply reflected and presented by Balarama Dasa. It has been accepted overtly by Balarama Dasa that as Lord Jagannath was his revered deity and it had become possible for him to compose such magnum opus like Ramayana. On several occasions, the poet has mentioned about the naming of the text in the name of Lord Jagannath and even mentioned that Lord Jagannath himself was the composer of his Ramayana. This can be corroborated by these verses-

"This Ramayana is Sri Jagamohana
Its poet is Nilagiri Jagannath"
[*Sri Jagamohana Ehi Ramayana*
Ethira kavi je Nilagiri Jagannath]

Though, many has termed his Ramayana as 'Dandi Ramayana' but he never mentioned at any place in his Ramayana as 'Dandi Ramayana'. He in a number of verses of Jagamohana Ramayana expressed his deepest devotion for Lord Jagannath. Many opined that as he had written his Ramayana by sitting near the *Jagamohana* of Puri Temple for which his work has been termed as Jagamohana Ramayana. Some opined that as it was written in *'dandi'* metre it was famous as Dandi Ramayana. Similarly, many other scholars have given their views about the name of Balarama Dasa's Ramayana but whatever may be the contentions it is famous as Jagamohana as he himself named it and most probably in honour of Lord Jagannath.

Before the time of Balarama Dasa and also during his time whatever religious sects and their concepts prevalent, he did not identify himself with any particular sect or faith or doctrine rather he had his own views and there was a union of all the theories and concepts in his composition and this unified divinity was the characteristic feature of the Panchasakhas. The poet was a worshipper of non-dualism within dualism concept, formless within the form and attributeless within attributes. He has given much importance to *jnana* (knowledge) and therefore accepted the concept of *jnana bhakti* (knowledge based on devotion). There is evidence in his writings regarding the characteristic feature of the doctrine of *sunya* (doctrine of void). Therefore, in his writing there is evidence of description of the doctrine of *jnana* (knowledge), *yoga*, *sunya* (void) and *bhakti* (devotion).

It is known from the Jagamohana Ramayana that the poet Balarama Dasa was a representative of Jagannath. There is a well-defined relationship between the incarnate and the incarnation. The poet has accepted the attributeless *brahma* i.e. Jagannath and the *brahma* with attribute i.e. Lord Rama as one and indivisible and identical. Thus, in his Ramayana at many places he described and addressed Rama as Brahma (Lord), Param Brahma (Supreme Lord), Maha Vishnu, Narayana, Jagannath etc. They all born to redress the sorrow of other deities in the Tretya Yuga and even a number of times there is mention of Goddess Lakshmi who born in the form of Sita on earth. The poet does not considered Rama as an ordinary incarnation rather he identified him with Narayana, Vishnu, Chakradhari, Chakrapani, Jagannath, Sri Hari, Vasudev, Janardhan, Daitari, Sripati, Kamalapati, Param Pususha, Paramananda Purusha, Anantakoti Brahmanda Adhipati, Sankha-Chakra-Gada-Padmadhari, Brahma, Param Brahma, Jagatkarta, Jagadisvara, Purusottama, Murari, Nara Hari, Govinda, Hrusikesha, Anadi, Viswanath, Banamali, Niranjana, Nirakara, Virat-Purusha, Brahma Murti, Brahmarasi etc.

The poet Balarama has accepted Lakshmana, Bharata, Satrughna as Vishnu himself as he considered them as part-incarnation of Vishnu because Lord Rama has taken birth in four forms. Balarama to indicate the devotion and reverence of Rama in Jagamohana Ramayana at several places emphasized upon chanting the name of Rama (Ramanama) and repeating the different names of Rama in his different incarnations. He started his work from the incantation of the name of Rama by Lord Siva. In his view-

"Prayers, sacrifices, pilgrimages all are sacred duties
If these are reproved all become vice and would be sin."

[*Japa, jajna, tirthabasa ate punyakarma*
Eha jhingasile papa atai adharma]

"Now Sadasiva do as I say,
Lessen your sin by repeating the name of Taraka brahma.
That by repeating the name of Rama all sins would go,
O! Siva recite Ramanama, debility would disappear,

You will obtain power and bliss and get everything

All your distress would go and you would become competent and capable." (Adikanda)

To the poet the name is more important than who holds it and the poet tried to prove it by making Rama to recite his own name (Ramataraka hymn) in the time of distress. At the time of war with Veerabahu and at the time of killing Ravana when he was nearer to become blind, Rama took the shelter of his own name. Among the gods, the creator Brahma, the protector Vishnu and the destroyer Siva all have remembered and uttered Ramanama. The poet has described at several places that he himself always recited Rmanama.

Lord Jagannath was the revered deity of the poet and as he considered Rama as a form of Jagannath he did not distinguish between Lord Jagannath and Rama. Lord Rama at the time of residing in the forest, the poet brought him to Nilachala Dhama to show him the wooden idol of Lord Jagannath and there he tried to depict the similarity between Ramachandra, Sita and Lakshmana with Jagannath, Subhadra and Baladev (Balabhadra).

The poet several times has shown his all out devotion towards Jagannath in his work. To show the greatness of Ramayana the poet indicated how by reading and hearing the tale of Rama all good happens and all round development occurs. In his words-

"For the delight of the sage I prepared the scripture

I composed Ramayana for the happiness of the world."

"I repeat it again and again for the benefit of my self

O Lord you be generous towards me."

"For the good of the world I translated it

As such provided virtuosity to the impious."

"Thus for the deliverance of the soul I did this

With great satisfaction I told the story of Rama."

It is known from the aforesaid depictions that poet Balarama revered Ramachandra as much as Lord Jagannath. By composing this Ramayana he played a crucial role in the propagation of the tale of Rama throughout Odisha. In the subsequent period by the influence of Jagamohan Ramayana a number of Ramakatha (tale of Rama) oriented poems, dramas were conceived which in the wake not only enriched the Odia literature but also led to the development of the Ramabhakti (devotion of Rama) in Odisha.

THE DESCANT

Balarama Dasa started his Ramayana by invoking Lord Jagannath. As a practice found in ancient scriptures, Balarama Dasa presented the Ramayana in the trend of speaker and listener tradition where he made Siva as the speaker and Parvati as listener. Not only at the inception of his work but throughout it he presented all events in a catechismal manner i.e. instruction drawn up by question and answer between Siva and Parvati. The Jagamohana Ramayana started with the worship of Ramanama. In the introduction he concisely discussed the tale of Satidaha (burning of Sati i.e. Parvati), destruction of Dakhya Yajna (the sacrificial ceremony of Daksha) etc. He discussed how Siva was etiolated by committing the sin of the destruction of that *yajna* and obstruction of the religious duty and he could not get his power until the wearing off the sins he committed. For that Brahma advised him to worship the name of Rama (Ramanama) among the thousand names of Vishnu (Vishnu Sahasranama) and Siva was relieved from his sins and got his earlier power and health. And it is at the request of Parvati to know about Rama in detail, Siva narrated the whole Ramayana to her.

In Jagamohana Ramayana there is mention of the tale of Rusyasrunga. In the royal court, Dasaratha has expressed his despair and sorrow due to the absence of any male offspring. Sage Vashistha consoled him. He got the news from Sumantra that Rusyasrunga has come to his friend King Lomapada of Champavati kingdom. From hearing about Rusyasrunga and to bringing him to Ayodhya and performing *Putresthi Yajna*, Balarama Dasa has described the events sequentially regarding the birth of Rusyasrunga, sending of a group of prostitutes under the young and beautiful Jaratkrusa, their voyage, the natural scene of the jungle besides the river valley, the mollification of Rusyasrunga by the young girls, taking him to Champavati in a boat, the welcoming of Rusyasrunga by Lomapada, Rusyasrunga's intelligent question to Lomapada and advising him on the administration of the kingdom, the meeting of Dasaratha with Rusyasrunga, the marriage of Rusyasrunga with Santa, sending of dowry to the hermitage (*ashrama*) of Bibhandaka, the compunction of Bibhandaka, his visit to Champavati, the blessing of Bibhandaka to Dasarath and Lomapada, birth of son of the sonless Lomapada by the *yajna* of Bibhandaka and Rusyasrunga, the coming of Rusyasrunga with Dasaratha to Ayodhya, the arrangement of *Putresti Yajna*, the invitation of kings of different kingdoms, coming of sages to Ayodhya at the invitation and the beginning of the *yajna* etc.

The main reason of the incarnation of Rama was the destruction of Ravana and his empire. The other two minor reasons of the incarnation were the liberation of Jaya and Vijaya from the malediction and fulfillment of the blessings given to Kasyapa and Aditi.

In the Uttara Kanda of Jagamohana Ramayana it has been mentioned that the porters, Jaya and Vijaya has to spent three life on earth as demon and human being. Balarama Dasa has described in the Uttara Kanda that due to the curse of sage Durbasa, Jaya and Vijaya in their first life would be born as Hiranya and Hiranaksha, in their second life they would be Ravana and Kumbhakarna and in their third life they would be born as Salva and Sisupala and they would get deliverance by the blow of weapon of Vishnu. At the time of telling the events of his previous birth to his queen Mandodari, Ravana told that Kumbhakarna and he were the porters of Vishnu. Due to the curse of Goddess Lakshmi they took birth as demons, Chanda and Prachanda. For their deliverance, they had to die by the blow of arrow of Rama, the incarnation of Vishnu. Therefore, Vishnu has incarnated himself as Rama for their liberation. Balarama Dasa in Jagamohana Ramayana has mentioned clearly that Dasaratha was the incarnation of Kasyap and Kausalya was that of Aditi. Vishnu as per his blessing took birth as their son and the avatar (incarnation) of Rama was one of the reasons.

Birth of Rama

After the completion of *Putresti Yajna*, Dasaratha had chosen, his three queens Kausalya, Kaikeyi and Sumitra out of seven hundred fifty queens to distribute equally the sacrificial pudding. Dasaratha told these three queens to observe a vow probably fasting to receive the sacrificial pudding. At the time when he distributed the pudding to Kausalya and Kaikeyi he was reminded about Sumitra and by confessing his mistake he requested the two queens to share their sacrificial pudding with Sumitra. At his request, each of them gave a part of their share to Sumitra and as such the pudding was divided in to four parts and Dasaratha became the father of four sons instead of one.

There is mention of the queens become pregnant after taking of the sacrificial pudding. He explained concisely but sufficiently the nature and symptoms of pregnant women, the various practices, rules and regulations to be followed during pregnancy. He mentions that Rama and other sons of Dasaratha were born on *Chaitra Sukla Navami* (ninth day of lunar fortnight of April). Then he described all the initial ceremonies usually observed after the birth of a child like- giving of alms, preparation of horoscope by the Brahmans, cutting of the umbilical cord, performing of different festivals like, *Sathi Puja*, *Navagraha Puja*, ceremony at the attainment of twenty-one days, naming ceremony and with the growing years the first shaving of the head, piercing of the ear, thread ceremony, initiation of learning, arms training etc.

Balarama Dasa followed sage Valmiki is evident from the fact that the incidents which are mentioned in the Valmiki Ramayana such as taking of Rama and Lakshmana by sage Viswamitra for the protection and safety of the *yajna* to their presence in Mithila all have been given place in Jagamohana Ramayana.

Ahalya

The tale of Ahalya has been discussed in detail in Jagamohana Ramayana. Brahma, the Creator by uniting all the beauties of the world has created a woman and named her as Ahalya. Her beauty attracted the gods, demons and humans alike who prayed Brahma to get her. Having no other way, Brahma told all to board on their respective vehicles and circumambulate the whole world thrice and whoever would succeeded in this he would give Ahalya to him. Therefore, all were indulged in a competition to acquire her. But, sage Gautama, who was proficient and well conversant in the *shastras* and law codes did not indulge in such a competition to get Ahalya. Brahma seeing him sitting quietly and phlegmatically asked him the reason for not competing with others to move around the world. At this, Gautama replied politely that when the cow named Suravi who holds nine earths and seven seas in her womb is with him there is no need to make unnecessary effort to go for a circumambulation of the earth thrice. Then he circled around Suravi thrice and then sat at the feet of Brahma. He was overwhelmed by seeing Gautama's humility and politeness, in-depth scriptural knowledge and ready wit and gave Ahalya to him. Being tempted by the beauty of Ahalya once the covetous Indra filled with unholy desire entered the *ashrama* of Gautama in his absence and prayed her to satisfy him by coition. Ahalya reproached Indra for this and at the time of returning from there, a mischievous idea struck to his mind. By seeing that Gautama has gone for ablutions and much time is there for his return, he again entered the *ahrama*, this time disguised as Gautama and approached Ahalya with solicitation. Ahalya was surprised to see the impersonated Indra in the form of Gautama returned so early and when asked the reason of his unusual early return, he replied that being smitten by the physical exposure of the bathing women, lust arose in him, so that he returned to her for coition. Therefore, the chaste Ahalya without hesitation readily yielded to his desire and engaged in physical union with him and Indra getting his eternally desired Ahalya engaged a longer time in copulating with her. The suddenly Indra realizing the return of Gautama, fled from there in the form of a cat and Ahalya repented her loss of judgment and the consequent misdeed. Gautama through his all seeing wisdom came to know the heinousness act of Indra and cursed him to become impotent and loose his manhood and be endowed with thousands of muliebre. Gautama also cursed Ahalya to become a stone. Then Indra out of shame went to Manasarovara and hide there in self-concealment. There was a large scale disorder in heaven due to the absence of Indra. Then at the request of Brahma, sage Gautama blessed Indra that his thousand muliebre be converted into thousand eyes and as such Indra came to be known as Sahasraksha (thousand eyed). Brahma went to Manasarovara and planted testicles of ram (male sheep) in Indra to remove his impotency. Balarama Dasa has also mentioned that Ramachandra before reaching Mithila freed Ahalya from the curse by the touching his feet and after a long wait and sage Gautama accepted her again.

Birth of Sita

In Jagamohana Ramayana, Sita has been described as earth born and she was nourished and brought up by king Janaka. As Balarama has accepted Ramachandra as the incarnation of Vishnu, therefore, he considered Sita as an incarnation of Goddess Lakshmi.

In his words, sage Viswamitra described about the birth of Sita to Rama and Lakshmana as such- desiring to get a son Janaka ploughed the chosen site for performing a *yajna*, and at that time, he saw nymph Menaka was passing over there in the sky to heaven after being freed from a curse. By being attracted to her beauty great desire arose in him to get a daughter like her. As Menaka was a nymph of heaven, she came to know the intention of Janaka and she told him that because of the curse of Brahma, she after spending a long time on the earth as a human being returning to heaven. Otherwise, she would have taken birth as his daughter. However, she told to him that there is no need to worry, as he would get a daughter a crore times more qualitative, virtuous and beautiful than herself. Then she told him to nurture her with much care and offer her to lord Vishnu. Therefore, at the time of ploughing the field meant for the *yajna* (sacrifice), the top of the plough touched an iron box and when it was unboxed, a child, divinely beautiful was found. Later when he came to know that she was self-born (*ajonija*), he brought up and nurtured her with great care.

Breaking of Siva's Bow

Balarama Dasa mentioned several times the topic of the breaking of the bow of Lord Siva. He described the history of the bow and also mentioned how king Janaka got this bow. Lord Siva himself created this bow in order to destroy the world after the self-immolation of Sati (wife of Siva) in the *yajna* performed by Daksha. Thence he gave it to the progenitor of Janaka, Nimiraja and at that time, Siva informed Nimiraja that Goddess Lakshmi would take birth in his family. Again here, the poet describes that at the time of Parasurama's meeting with Rama he told the latter about this bow that earlier Viswakarma built two bows and one he gave to Vishnu and the other to Siva. Then Siva gave his bow to the ancestor of Janaka, Devarata. Likewise Vishnu gave his bow to sage Ruchika and as the grandson of sage Ruchika he himself is carrying it as Parasurama. The bow which was broken by Rama was that of Lord Siva.

When Ramachandra lifted the bow from the iron bow-case, Lakshmana requested the *Digpala* (keeper of the horizon), Vasuki (the serpent who holds the earth), Mahakurma (the great Tortoise) and Vasumati (the earth) to remain steady. Vasumati expressed her inability to bear the weight of the bow and requested distressfully to Rama not to keep the pointed end of the bow on her. Ramachandra in his all assuming form (*Viswarupa*) lifted the bow resting its pointed end on the little finger of his left feet and when he was about to string it , the bow prayed to him not to revile it by destroying its virility. Ramachandra consoled the bow and told it that it has become very old and when it was in the hands of Siva it was used by him to destroy the three worlds and as such vicariously it was also a party to the sin committed by Siva. Therefore, Ramachandra assured the bow to make it sinless by destroying it and by which it would attain salvation. By hearing this, the bow got great satisfaction. Consequently, when Ramachandra strung the bow, it was broken into two pieces. In his description of the events from *Dhanuryajna* of Janaka to Dasaratha's visit to Mithila by hearing the news of the breaking of the bow, the poet has proven his poetic magnificence in his contextual descriptions related to the bow and established the originality of his inimitable conceptions.

Marriage Ceremony

In Jagamohana Ramayana before the breaking of the bow, the love of Sita for Rama was unfolded. While sitting on the golden platform with her friends, Sita was frightened by seeing the gigantic bow. Suspicion arose in her mind as to how it would be lifted and stringed by a young lad when the mighty and powerful warriors present there failed miserably. However, she became hopeful after being consoled by her friends and at such a time, Ramachandra stepped out to lift the bow effortlessly and tied the string on it. When the friend of Sita identified Rama to her, she was fascinated by his personality and she prayed to god to get him as her husband. At this time, her left eyelid started throbbing, which was considered as an auspicious sign, and there were many such weal and woe incidents happened which prompted Sita to think that her desire is going to be fulfilled. Ultimately, after the breaking of the bow by Ramachandra, Sita was delighted by offering him the garland.

Thereafter when Ramchandra denied to get marry in the absence of his father, Janaka decided to send priest Satananda to Ayodhya. Ramchandra has written a long letter and send it with Satananda. Janaka from his side offered with eagerness his two daughters and the two daughters of Kushadhwaja to the four sons of Dasaratha. Satananda after reaching Ayodhya delivered the letter of Rama to Dasaratha, who after reading it delightedly praised Rama. Thereafter, king Dasaratha along with the ministers, the sages, queens began the journey towards Mithila. After reaching there, Dasaratha insisted Kushadhwaja to come to Mithila with his two daughters. Then after ascertaining an auspicious time marriage was arranged. Balrama Dasa has described in detail the customs that were followed in conducting the marriage which have a local tinge. Dasaratha at the time of returning to Ayodhya with his sons and daughter-in-laws Janaka had given many advises to Sita.

Encounter with Parasurama

Dasaratha returned to Ayodhya with much pomp and gaiety, by beating of drums and with procession and at this time they passed through the Siddhivana where the hermitage of Parasurama existed. Rama's procession had broken the meditation and penances of Parasurama, the sworn enemy of the Kshatriyas. He had not tolerated the drumbeat and came out in anger and obstructed the way of Dahatatha. By seeing the awe-inspiring attire of Parasurama, Dasaratha was frightened and requested Vasishtha to save him from this dangerous situation and when Vasishtha along with Viswamitra about to approach Parasurama, the latter himself came to see them and they also were frightened to see his terrible appearance. Dasaratha tried again and again to pursue and convince him but in vain. Parasurama derided Dasaratha for the grand procession which disturbed him and at the same time wanted to see the person for whom such procession being carried out. Then when he was ready to blow Rama with his axe, Dasaratha, Vasishtha, Viswamitra all requested him to calm down. Parasurama told Rama the history of the bow of Siva and of the bow of Vishnu in his hand and also informed him about the annihilation of many generation of Kshatriyas. To judge and examine the strength of Rama, he challenged him for a duel. But, Rama expressed his unwillingness to engage in such a scuffle and told him that he usually do not fight with revered persons. Due to his defiant and truculent attitude, Rama told him that if he would not have an old Brahmin and someone else he would have given him a condign punishment. At such a reply, Parasurama in anger put forward the bow of Vishnu and asked him to string the bow considering that because of the heaviness of the bow, Rama would fall on the ground and die. However, to his dismay Rama strung the bow and set the arrow on it, drew the string with ease and all the pride of Parasurama was decimated. Rama at the time of receiving the bow from Parasurama had taken away his radiance and remitted his sins by the arrow which he has set on the bow. Parasurama became aware of the existence and divinity of Rama and thus gave his bow and the imperishable quiver to Rama and departed from there for penitence.

Balarama Dasa with the description of the return of Dasaratha to Ayodhya and observance of festivals there and the other related activities ended his Adi Kanda. He not only followed Valmiki Ramayana at the same time he also accepted different new tales from various scriptures and presented them unitedly in his work. Though the above mentioned incidents were written by following the Valmiki Ramayana, Balarama Dasa's credit is that he combined with them his own imagination and presented them with a style of his own.

Ayodhya Kanda

By seeing that Rama was endowed with all round qualities and his popularity among the subjects, Dasaratha had decided to make him his successor and coronate him as the crown prince. He also got wholehearted support of the family preceptor, Vasishtha, the eminent and erudite sages, the ministers etc. who ratified in one voice delightedly Ramachandra's elevation to the position of crown prince. Here it is quite interesting to note the style of elucidation of Balarama Dasa. In his words- by hearing the coronation of Rama, Manthara, the women companion and confidential servant of queen Kaikeyi on the royal road itself expressed her mental reaction and started quarreling with the people. Suffused with anger she rushed to the harem of Kaikeyi and fell down by becoming senseless. When she regained her consciousness by the personal care of Kaikeyi she immediately conveyed her the bad news that Rama is being made the crown prince of Ayodhya. By hearing, this Kaikeyi in great delight gave Manthara some valuable pearl necklaces and promised to give her more ornaments if this would really happen. She became restless in joy and delight. As much as Manthara had given bad counseling to her like, if Rama would become king in future how the prominence and predominance of Sita and Kaushalya would increase etc. did not have any impact on the mind of the simple and uncorrupted Kaikeyi. This fathomless motherly love of Kaikeyi for Rama, created problem among the gods. By considering that the death of Ravana would be impossible if Rama would become king and thus to create disruptions they sent to earth– *Khala* (the wicked) and *Durbala* (the weak). The *Khala* resided in the heart of Kaikeyi and the *Durbala* resided in the heart of Dasaratha. Now the gods were assured that at the instigation of Weak and the Wicked both Kaikeyi and Dasaratha would be guided and behave accordingly. Thus, Kaikeyi succumbs to the evil counseling of Manthara and gradually started to believe her words. Then she questioned Manthara as to how the younger Bharata would be made king instead of the elder brother Rama by Dasaratha . Saraswati, the Goddess of Eloquence present in the throat of Manthara, uttered in the voice of the latter reminding Kaikeyi about the two boons she supposed to get from Dasaratha. To get these promises she first made Dasaratha to swear for the fulfillment of his boons. By the first boon, she asked for the crowning of Bharata and by the second one, she asked for the exile of Rama into the forest. Kaikeyi tried to ward off the hither and thitherness of king Dasaratha to fulfill his promises by explaining him the importance of truth and also the munificence of Siva and king Vali.

Balarama Dasa also mentioned one incident associated with Kaikeyi which is like this- earlier when Kaikeyi was unmarried once an old anchorite having matted lock of grey hair and loose skin visited the court of his father. Kaikeyi laughed at him loudly in an insulting manner for his appearance and at such gesture of her the ascetic cursed her that the way she ridiculed him, one day the whole world will hate and ridicule her. As a result of this curse for sending Rama to the forest, she was hated and ridiculed by all.

Balarama Dasa mentioned in relation to Manthara that she was the incarnation of Devamata (Gomata) Suravi. She was created as a maidservant of Kaikeyi by the gods for being another succourer for the destruction of Ravana. She had a hunch on her back for which she was called hunched back woman. As per the providential arrangement, Manthara by her ill advise to Kaikeyi sent Rama to forest. The poet also described Manthara's attitude of revenge. At his marriage ceremony at Mithila as Rama insulted her in front of all, she avenged it by making him punished with exile.

Kaikeyi's obstinacy and Rama's march to forest

Dasaratha had gone into a state of deep consternation after hearing the demands of Kaikeyi and became speechless. Kaikeyi did not receive any answer from him and she decided to return to her father's house leaving Ayodhya. At this time when there was delay in the coronation of Rama, Sumantra and other ministers along with Vasishtha went to Dasaratha and questioned about Rama's coronation but they did not receive any answer. They were stunned and astounded to hear from Kaikeyi about Bharata's elevation to the position of crown prince and Rama's exile, which has been agreed upon by Dasaratha himself. Even Vasishtha and Vamadeva came to know by meditating that without Rama's exile into the forest the demise of Ravana is impossible, still they expressed their sorrow for the ugly turn of the events.

When Kausalya came to know from Rama about his exile into forest, she explained to Rama the mythological event of the birth of Pavan (Air) and turning Pavan into pieces by Indra in the womb of his mother and requested him not to leave Ayodhya even if he did not get the kingdom. At such speech of the mother, Rama tried to counter and convince her by giving example of the importance of the observance of the promise of the father by Parasurama. In a similar manner he was also resolved and determined to fulfill the words of the father. Lakshmana vehemently protested this and even went to the extent of telling that he is prepared to kill Kaikeyi, Bharata and Satrughna and hand over the kingdom to Rama by making it thorn less and unrivalled. He reproached his henpecked father.

When Rama went to Sita for bidding farewell and told her about his exile to the forest, Sita also expressed her desire to be his companion in his journey. And Balarama Dasa described that she threatened if she would not be taken she would consume poison. Lakshmana also got the permission to go along with Rama and Sita. Thereafter, when the three- Rama, Lakshmana and Sita bid adieu to Dasaratha, Kaikeyi had distributed two pieces of cloth to each along with beads of rosary (*Rudraksha*), basil rosary and earring for which Dasaratha reviled her harshly. At this time, Rama pacified him and at Dasaratha's direction, Sumantra brought many good clothes and ornaments for Sita, but Rama and Lakshmana received the clothes and other articles given by Kaikeyi and bid adieu in the attire of ascetics.

Rama and Guhyaka and Rama's visit to Chitrakuta

In the Jagamohana Ramayana, the poet told about the hunting practices of Rama and Lakshmana. At the time of hunting Rama, Lakshmana and the assisting soldiers were separated from each other. The enervated hunter Rama, having lost his way while taking rest on the bank of river Tamasa, he met Guhyaka who also came for hunting and Rama became a friend with him. Guhyaka was a son of a hunter Biradha. At this time, Lakshmana and others arrived there and Rama departed from Guhyaka and returned to Ayodhya.

When Ramachandra had been to forest, he stayed for some time at Srungaberpur and by receiving the news of Rama's stay, Guhyaka met him. Poet Balarama has described Guhyaka as the chief of the hunter class (*Sabaras*) and nowhere described him as a Chandala (a lower caste). He has given a flawless detailed description of the dress and ornaments, practices, customs, usages of the hunter race of Odisha. When Guhyaka heard about the entire episode of how Dasaratha at the instance of Kaikeyi sent Rama to forest out of anger he sought permission from Rama to decapitate Dasaratha and Kaikeyi and bring Bharata and Satrughna as captive, but Rama placated him. At the request of Guhyaka, Rama, Lakshmana and Sita spent the night there. When Rama, Lakshmana, Sumantra were in conversation in the night, Rama at the request of Lakshmana told about how the parrot and *myna* (a kind of sterling) got reprieve from the hawk. It appears that this description is poet Balarama's own creation. In the following morning, Ramachandra after completion of his morning duties began his journey. The boats man of the boat arranged by Guhyaka by hearing that at the touch of Rama's feet a stone turned into a woman did not agree to ferry Rama in his boat because the boat was the only means of his livelihood. But, later he was convinced and after washing the feet of Rama he took him in his boat.

Balarama Dasa had maintained the seriatim of the subject matter in proper perspectives throughout and tried to provide it an attractive form through his prolonged discussion of various events. At the time of crossing river Ganga, Rama prayed Ganga. After crossing the river his indulgence in hunting, his plunging in to the thinking about Ayodhya and the ministering of Lakshmana with loving words of courage and love, his entering into the hamlet of Savaras, the praise of them by the inhabitants of the hamlet, Sita's conversation with the women there, all these have been discussed in detail by the poet. Then he described the visit of Rama, Lakshmana and Sita to the *ashrama* of sage Bharadwaj at Prayag (Triveni Sangam). Bharadwaj advised Rama to return to Ayodhya. But, by seeing the firmness of Rama to keep the words of his father and by knowing through meditation that the death of Ravana depends on Rama's exile into the forest, he advised Rama to stay at the demon infested Chitrakuta. He had given a thorough topographical instruction of the region and admonished him to remain cautious all the time. By spending the night at the *ashrama* in the following morning Rama, Lakshmana and Sita set out for Chitrakuta by crossing the river Kalindi (Yamuna). They reached Chitrakuta and en-route the poet described Sita's offering of prayers under the Banchabata (the big banyan tree that fulfils the desires) and Rama's hunting session. Then to describe the natural beauty of Chitrakuta, the poet has described the picturesque beauty of the forest regions of Odisha.

Union of Rama and Bharata

Dasaratha after describing about the incident of the curse of the blind sage to Kausalya gone into deep sleep and the grief stricken Dasaratha died when he was in deep slumber without the knowledge of Kausalya. When he had not replied to her question about the virtue and excellence of Rama, she assumed that he was asleep. In the morning when the demise of Dasaratha was unfolded except Kaikeyi all the queens bewailed. When Bharata and Satrughna returned from his maternal uncle's house and they came to know about the happenings from Kaikeyi, Bharata derided and rebuked her in strong words and got ready to kill Manthara whom he considered solely responsible for the ugly turn of the events. At this time at the request of the Gods and the Goddesses, Saraswati resided in Satrughna who advised Bharata to desist from committing the sin of killing a woman. Both reproached Manthara for her damning activities.

The poet described all the incidents from Bharata establishing his innocence near Kausalya to his presence in Chitrakuta, Rama's lesson of Rajadharma to Bharata, Rama and Sita's offering of obsequial oblation to Dasaratha, Rama, Lakshamana and Sita's meeting with the mothers, Bharata's failure to bring back Rama and his protest by sleeping on the grass spread, sending of sandal in the hands of the disciple of sage Sarabhanga to Rama, return of Bharata to Ayodhya with the sandals of Rama.

Aranya Kanda

Balarama Dasa in his epic after prolonged obeisance to Baladeva started the narration of his Aranya Kanda.

Bharata after returning from Chitrakuta did not enter Ayodhya and he established the sandals of Rama at Nandigrama and ruled the kingdom from there. When the sages decided to leave Chitrakuta, Rama asked the reason of their abandonment of the *ashrama* to which they replied that they did not want to confront the demons. They blamed Rama for this vicariously. Because the presence of Rama and Lakshmana would send a message to the demons that, the sages engaged two archers for their destruction. As much as Ramachandra tried to convince them for not to leave Chitrakuta, they had not acccpted his explications. Thereafter, Rama, Lakshmana and Sita also left Chitrakuta and travelled through the Dakshinapatha.

Then the poet described Rama's visit to the *ashrama* of sage Atri and Anasuya, theirs spending the night in the *ashrama*, the advises of Atri about them, about the way of living in the forest, his words of caution to Rama to remain attentive in the demon infested forest, his advice to them to stay in the beautiful Dandakaranya etc. in detail.

Then the poet described the incident that Indra by being anxious about the terrible penance of sage Mandakarna, sent the daughters of Panchakanya to earth. By singing songs they were able to break his penance and after sage Mandakarna came to know about them, he took them with him and built a beautiful abode under the water of a lake and since then he has been listening songs there.

Balarama through his description took Ramachandra to Ganga. After describing the greatness and utility of offering oblation at Ganga, he told about the event of Ramachandra's offering of obsequial cake to his ancestors. At this time due to impurity, Sita was unable to offer oblation with Rama and out of shame she in the pretension of playing prepared funeral cakes with the sands of river Phalgu and offer it to Dasaratha by uttering his name and *gotra*. Even if Sita offered it in amusement, Dasaratha accepted it with his hands and his soul attained heaven. Later when Ramchandra as per rules and customs offered the obsequious cake this was not accepted by the soul of the deceased Dasaratha as his soul has already attained the final salvation. The Gods informed him that there is no need to offer it again as Dasaratha obtained heaven at Sita's offering of sand cakes. Ramachandra to verify the truth asked Phalgu about it but, Phalgu at the request of Sita denied it and at this Ramchandra cursed Phalgu to become waterless. As a result of which from that day no water is found in Phalgu except rain water. But, Sita due to the innocence and inoffensiveness of Phalgu showed compassion and blessed her by which water would be visible by the slightest digging of the sands of Phalgu and henceforth even now it is a belief in vogue that by offering obsequious cake prepared in sands of Phalgu, the ancestors accepts them cordially and respectfully.

Then the poet describes vividly in his idiosyncratic style the oppression of the Brahmins at the platforms and the consequent curse of Rama to the Brahmins. Then Rama went to Kasi. There also due to the oppressive attitude of Brahmins he cursed them.

Then Rama, Lakshmana and Sita by crossing river Narmada and Punyabhadra reached Chandrabhaga. There, after taking bath and offering oblations they moved in the southward direction and established Ramachandi and Pasanachandi respectively. Then after taking bath in the holy Bindusagar tank visited Ekamratirtha. On the way, he took shelter in a number of monasteries and asylums and finally reached Purusottama. Rama, Lakshmana and Sita saw Jagannath, Balabhadra and Subhadra. Then they journeyed towards the south. On the bank of Rusikulya they visited the Gods and Goddesses in Akshatesvar, Kulaichandi, Bilunkesvar. He by breathing life in to the bowl of white gourd consecrated Lord Siva in the name of Tumbesvar. Then the poet concisely referring the curse of a sage to the king of Dandaka, took Rama to the hermitage of sage Sutikhna in Dandakaranya. After staying there for one month Rama, Lakshmana and Sita had taken leave from Sutikhna and begun their journey towards the *ashrama* of sage Agasti. After taking advice from Agasti, Rama, Lakshmana and Sita went towards Panchavati. On the way, they came across Marich in the guise of a golden stag that obstructed their way. When Rama set his arrow towards him, he ran away but two of his associates dies. In Panchavati, Rama met Jatayu and he was delighted by knowing that Jatayu was a friend of his father. They built cottages and spent times in joy and happiness by hunting and feasting fruit meals.

Purloin of Sita

In the Jagamohana Ramyana, the poet as usual followed the events of the Valmiki Ramayana but his own style and some uniqueness can be visible. In the context of the episode of Sita's purloin he describes-

After hearing from his sister Surpanakha about the exquisite beauty of Sita, Ravana's desire was kindled and he became very restive to get her every now and then. By seeing her mental state and his unsteadiness, Mandodari, the queen consort of Ravana asked the reason of his perplexity. Ravana told her everything. After hearing the whole incident, Mandodari advised Ravana not to indulge in such wicked and evil deed. But, Ravana turned a deaf year to her good counseling. Then Ravana set out on his Chariot and went in the northerly direction and arrived near deceptive Maricha. He presented his plan near Maricha by which the latter was frightened and pleaded for the good for Ravana and told about the heroism of Rama but Ravana had not heeded him as he was impelled by a lustful desire to possess Sita.

At last, Maricha agreed to the proposal of Ravana and transformed him into a wonderful deer. Sita became spell bound to see the disguised stag and called Rama and Lakshmana to see the wondrous beauty. She persuaded Rama to catch it for her. Rama set out for capturing the stag and cautioned Lakshmana to remain by Sita's side and guard her vigilantly. When Maricha took Rama far out then Rama being tired of the pursuit sent forth an arrow and Maricha died feigning Rama's voice shouting the name of Sita and Lakshmana. Sita was deceived and in agony and anxiety compelled Lakshmana to go for the help of Rama. Lakshmana was aware of the wiles of the demons and as much as he tried to convince Sita, she was not in a position to listen any consolation. The poet has described that Lakshmana unwillingly went but before that he drawn three lines at the entrance of the hut and cautioned Sita not to transgress these lines.

The poet has displayed his own style in the description of the transformation of Ravana into a mendicant ascetic uttering Vedic hymns. To express his feelings near Sita the way Ravana passed remarks about her which were nothing else but vulgarity. Ravana had not wanted anything from Sita except her love. Therefore, he forcibly abducted Sita and the Gods rejoiced in exaltation and started preparation for song and dance in heaven. At the order of Brahma, Narad went to Panchavati to verify the veracity of the fact that whether Sita was purloined by Ravana or not. The Gods had concluded by counting that there are eleven months and a fortnight to go for the death of Ravana. They by thinking that the curse of Nandi, Rambha and Vedavati to Ravana are going to be fulfilled shortly were delighted. At the time of Ravana's engagement in war with Jatayu, the escaping of Sita through the forest path has been beautifully depicted by the poet. Then by following Sita's footprints and sound of crying, Ravana discovered her from the place of self concealment and carried away her to Lanka by the aerial way. The citizens of Lanka were stunned by the charm and uncommon beauty of Sita. After keeping Sita in Asokavana, Ravana presented many expensive gifts to her and politely requested her to accept him as her husband. He exhibited to Sita his inner feelings as how he has been immersed in the ocean of her beauty. But as Sita remained silent without any reply to his offer, by indicating the Rakshasis to make all out efforts to break her obstinacy and arouse love and attachment towards him he returned to the palace.

Search for Sita

The absence of Sita in the *ashrama* perturbed Rama and Lakshmana. The worried Rama was consoled by Lakshmana and they went out in search of Sita. On their way they came across Kabandha which means barrel shaped one whose body was deformed by the curse of sage Sthulagriv and after Rama set him free from the curse, he advised Rama to set out towards a lake named Pampa. On the way, Rama felt thirsty and to quench his thirst, Lakshmana shot his arrow and pierced the mountain and made the water flow from Patala Ganga. Later the stream of water turned into a lake named as Lakshmana Hrada. The following day Rama and Lakshmana after taking bath in the river Tungabhadra worshipped the Virupaksha Linga and then they reached the cottage of Sabari on the bank of river Pampa. Sabari respectfully and generously treated them by offering them fruits gathered and tested by her. Rama was greatly satisfied by her hospitality. By accepting the orts fruits from her, Ramachandra had made the popular conception "God is of the devotee" meaningful. The poet has beautifully depicted the episode of the interaction between Sabari and Ramachandra and the subsequent deliverance of the former. Sabari advised Ramachandra to go to Rysyamuka and where he would be able to rescue Sita with the help of Sugriva. Then she transformed into a beautiful form and ascended to heaven.

Balarama Dasa has beautifully mentioned various events after Rama's entry into the Rusyamuka sauch as- the wonderful description of the lake Pampa in the autumn, the thought and reminiscence and lamentation of Rama for Sita, the poet's invocation of goddess Durga, the long conversation between Rama and Lakshmana on the bank of Pampa. Rama enquired about Sita to Chakravaka (Ruddy Sheldrake) and Chakravaki (Female Ruddy Sheldrake) present there. But, Chakravaka's reproach to Rama for creating obstruction in their copulation which infuriated Lakshmana and he imprecated Chakravaka-Chakravaki. Then Chakravaka importunately prayed to Rama to forgive and Rama consoled him. When Chakravaka and Chakravaki were captured by the bird catcher, the door of the cage opened on its own in the evening due to Rama's blessing and both of them got freedom. Rama and Lakshmana felt hungry and Rama requested the cowherds to provide milk to them in exchange of a ring, but the mischievous cowherds ridiculed them and at such behaviour, Lakshmana cursed them for not providing milk and the milk turned into blood. Then the cowherd realizing their fault prayed Rama to forgive them and provided them with milk. Rama blessed the cowherds and promised them to take birth as one of their child in the next life.

The poet utilized all the opportunities, advantages and conveniences at his disposal to make his work heart touching and attractive. His style of presentation and excellent exposition is a proof of that which not only proved his poesy but also depicted his all encompassing character of a poet, narrator, devotee which were the magnanimities of the age of the Panchasakhas.

Kiskindha Kanda

After the purloin of Sita by Ravana from the point of view of the course of events, the subject matter of this Kanda bears importance because Ramachandra as a dexterous administrator concentrated all his thought, knowledge and attention on the rescue operation of Sita and for that matter he established friendship with Sugriva and killed Vali. Friendship with Sugriva, killing of Vali, dispatching of the monkey force to locate Sita are the prominent theme of this Kanda.

Poet Balarama Dasa after elongate invocation of Agni, through the interaction between Siva and Parvati has started the narration of this Kanda.

The fugitive Vanara King Sugriva by seeing Rama and Lakshmana roving on the bank of Pampa presumed them as two bow-bearing ascetics sent by Vali, escaped to the tip of the Rusyamuka Mountain without informing his faithful adherents. His retinues went in search of him and discovered him from self-concealment in the cave of the mountain for fear of Vali. He told them about the spies of Vali and started crying by holding his head. At this time he was consoled by Hanuman who advised him to clandestinely collect all the information. Sugriva requested Hanuman to go incognito and ascertain their objective and purpose. Hanuman taking the form of a Brahmana met Rama and Lakshmana who were resting under a tree. When he wanted to know about them, Lakshmana had concisely given their introduction and explained their miserable story to Hanuman. Thence, when the moment Lakshmana asked about the identity of the disguised Hanuman, he was able to remember the earlier events. He had given the short introduction of Vali and Sugriva and told the deplorable condition of Sugriva because of Vali and introduced himself as an associate of Sugriva. Then he resumed his own form and at the query of Rama he explained how he got the crown, ear ring and the necklace of nine gems. He as per the words of Brahma regained his earlier prowess and valour. Then he went to Sugriva and conveyed to him the good news and at the instance of Suriva welcomed Rama and Lakshmana. When Sugriva asked them about the reason of the exile, Rama gave a short introduction and explained the other incidents to him. As both of them were displaced, crestfallen, loser of wives, and both of them were Suryavamsis, a friendship was established between them. They resolved to help and cooperate each other.

When conversing with Rama, Sugriva informed him about the prowess of Vali. He told him that whoever will cut seven palm trees (Saptasal), he alone would be able to kill Vali and this is what Surya said to him. Where Indra was unable to split one palm tree, Vali can split three such trees at once with an iron arrow. As Vali knows that his life is associated with the Saptasal and as he is aware of the fact that if he could split the Saptasal, he along with the ascetics would become immortal, he always tries to achieve success. The Saptasal is like an enemy of him because as per sage Durvasa's curse whoever would pierce it would kill Vali. After divulging the secret of Vali's death, Sugriva at Rama's query explained to him the reason of differences between them. Firstly, the description of Riksharaja's birth episode, turning of Riksharaja into a woman and the attraction of Vasava and Surya towards her, birth of Vali from the hair and Sugriva from the neck of Riksharaja because of falling of Vasava's semen on the hair and Aditya's sperm on the neck of the menstruated Riksharaja, coming of Brahma at the request of Vasava and Aditya to the Parvativana and taking of the two monkey faced babies by Riksharaja to the bank of river Gautami at Dandakaranya and leaving them there at the instance of Brahma, discovering of the two babies in helpless condition by Ahalya who had been to there for bath, coming of sage Gautama to the river bank and perceiving of Gautama through meditation about the events leading to the birth of these self born babies and taking them to his *ashrama*, coming of the king of Kishkindha to Dandakaranya and his meeting with sage Gautama and taking the babies at the direction of Gautama for nurturing them, performing of the marriage of Vali with Tara and Sugriva with Roma, Vali getting of the kingship of Kishkindha after the demise of the king etc. has been described by Sugriva.

Balarama Dasa to depict the causes of differences between Vali and Sugriva narrated the events as such- Once a demon named Mayavi came at the midnight and challenged Vali for a combat. Vali rushed forth immediately. But he fled from there after being hit by the fisticuff of Vali and described the insulting defeat to his younger brother Dunduvi. Then to avenge the defeat of his elder brother, Dunduvi went to fight with Vali. He was also defeated and persuaded by Vali who fled the battleground in the form of a buffalo for fear of life but Vali pounded him to death. And when he flung the dead buffalo to a long distance, drops of blood of Dundubhi's body were carried by the wind fell on the *ashrama* of sage Matanga when he was engaged in penances at Rusyamuka and in wroth he pronounced a curse on Vali thereby imprecating him for desecrating the holy spot and prohibiting him not to enter the precinct of the *ashrama* in Rusyamuka else he would lose his life. On hearing the death of Dundubhi Mayavi returned to Kishkindha with anger and started his oppressive activities there and challenged Vali again to which Vali responded forthwith by impetuously rushing to confront him, but fearing him Mayavi in the form of a bull entered into a cave through which he went to hell and Vali also pursuing him plunged into the cave. Sugriva as per the words given to Vali waited for long with his soldiers at the entrance but Vali did not come out. When he was in doubt all of sudden he heard sounds of groans and saw blood oozing out of the cave which made him sure that Vali had died in the struggle by the united attacks of the demons. Sugriva out of fear blocked the entrance of the cave with a huge rock returned Kishkindha with great sorrow and pain. He at the persuasion of elders and ministers accepted the vacant throne. When the coronation ceremony was going on Vali entered Kishkindha and drove out Sugriva who was in kingly attire, Hanuman who was holding the royal umbrella, Taraksha who was holding the chowrie, Susena who was holding the staff and Gandhamardan who was holding the royal sword from the court. The unfortunate Sugriva was thus deprived of his kingdom and even his wife and seek asylum in the Rusyamuka with some of his faithful retinues.

Ramachandra to dispel the doubts of Sugriva and create hope and confidence in him by a flip of his feet sent the enormous skeletons of Dundubhi to *satayojana* (hundreds of kilometers) and pierced the Saptasal (seven palm trees) and the Rusyamuka Mountain at once with his arrow. Sugriva was petrified at such unprecedented display of prowess. He begged pardon to Rama for examining his power out of ignorance. Thence at the advice of Rama, he challenges Vali for a duel.

The Slaying of Vali and Accession of Sugriva

As per the decision when Sugriva went to the lion gate of the palace and challenged Vali, the citizens of Kishkindha stared at him astonishingly. Vali also contemptuously laughed by hearing the vociferous challenge of Sugriva. He came out of his palace and grounded him by one thunder like fisticuff. Sugriva escaped from there to Rusyamuka and slept in the cave of the mountain in gloom and despair. Rama had consoled the woebegone Sugriva. When Rama contended that because of the similarity of appearance of the two, he did not set his arrow targeting Vali out of bewilderment. Then only Sugriva left his haughtiness and told Rama that unless he would recuperate from the bodily pain he is unable to fight again with Vali. Then Ramachandra by caressing with his hands on the body of Sugriva relieved him of his pain. And he was again ready to fight with all his vigour with the strength of a hundred lions. This time he put a garland in his neck as a mark of distinction from Vali.

When Vali was resting after dinner, Sugriva again challenged him in front of the lion gate of Kishkindha. Vali heard this from the harem. When he was readying himself to go outside to give Sugriva a condign punishment, his wife Tara restricted him not to pay heed to the challenge of Sugriva fearing foul play. She told Vali that she received the news from the scouts about the formation of a friendship between Rama and Sugriva. She also informed him that Ranachandra has resolved to kill him and handover the kingdom to Sugriva. She has also a bad dream regarding such a mishappening. She tried to convince the impetuous Vali by explaining a picture of her impending widowhood and repeatedly requested him not to go for a fight. But Vali tried to console her by saying that who is Rama? And why he would kill him without any fault of him? Even if Rama would kill him in order to give the kingdom to Sugriva, as a Kshatriya he cannot avert the call for a fight after hearing a challenge. By saying this, he marched ahead for the duel. Rama sped a deadly arrow towards Vali, which pierced his chest, and he fell down on the ground.

` Finding Rama near him Vali wanted to know his identity and questioned him why he had killed him causeless while he had no enmity with him. Rama told Vali about him, the reason of his exile, and the abduction of Sita by Ravana. Vali reproached Rama by saying that he is the son of Emperor Dasaratha and being born of a noble race of the righteous Raghuvamsa why he had committed this ignoble deed perfidiously. It is unbecoming of his reputation. He told that if it were for Sita he would have rescued her back without any difficulty from the clutch of Ravana as he knows the power of Ravana. Rama in order to repeal the accusations of Vali presented before him a number of logical arguments and requested him not to find fault with his actions. Vali at last was satisfied by the representations of Rama and also fully understood that Rama was the incarnation of Parambrahma. By applauding the excellence of Hanuman, Susena, Taraksha and Gandhamardan, he told Rama with hope that with their assistance he can succeed in rescuing Sita from Ravana. He advised Rama to always accept the advice of Jambavan and requested him to show mercy to Angad. He ordered Sugriva to serve Rama and help him without negligence in the operation to rescue Sita. He took out his necklace given to him by Indra and gave it to Sugriva. After that when death comes closer, he requested Rama to take out the arrow and emancipate him and the moment Rama took out the arrow, Vali died vomiting blood.

After getting the news of the death of Vali, Tara along with her seven sons arrived at the battlefield to have a last view of him. The ministers and courtiers also reached there. They requested Tara to order them to kill Rama, Lakshmana and Sugriva along with his followers in order to avenge the death of their king. At this time, Angad consoled them by telling that earlier he was informed by sage Gautama about the death of his father at the hands of Rama, the incarnation of Vishnu and bestowing of the kingdom to the paternal uncle. Therefore, Angad prevented them not to go against Lord Vishnu.

Tara bewailed plaintively at the death of Vali and cursed Rama for his act. However, later beseeched at the feet of Rama and requested him not to find fault with her behaviour and Rama pardoned her and blessed her to remain as a married woman for all time to come. She married Sugriva and as before became the queen consort. At the direction of Rama the body of Vali was cremated and the exequies were performed as per the customs and with due ceremony. After the coronation of Sugriva and Angad became the crown prince, Rama gave many advises to Sugriva about administration and went with Lakshmana to Malyabanta Mountain.

Search for Sita

Balarama Dasa depicted the natural beauty of Malyabanta Mountain during the rainy season. At the lamentation and discomfiture of Rama for the separation of Sita, Lakshmana counseled him and assured him to rescue Sita by killing Ravana within three months. Here the poet in the pretext of conversation between Hara and Parvati in order to describe evidently about the ignorance of Rama discussed the tale of Raja Marut. Through charity and virtuous acts and by performing *Aswamedha* sacrifice king Marut got a beautiful daughter named Leelavati. When she was young once, Narad and sage Parvat visited the palace of Marut and after seeing Leelavati they were overwhelmed by her beauty. Consequently, both of them expressed their desire to get her as wife. Then king Marut fell in contradiction as how to give his only daughter to the two sages. The following day he decided that as per her own desire if Leelavati chooses any one of them, he would give her to him. In the mean time, Lord Vishnu by knowing that the two sages being fascinated by seeing the Lakshmi like Leelavati, he himself decided to accept her. The following day mounting on Garuda, Lord Vishnu grant an audience to Leelavati and the latter wished to get Vishnu as her husband and put the garland around his neck. After that when Vishnu took her to heaven, Narad and sage Parvat being bashful about the turn of events considered Marut as conspirator and at the time of their return cursed him to get swallowed by ignorance. Then Marut seek refuge near Vishnu to make him free from the curse. Vishnu considering that the curse of the two sages was actually due to him and therefore the curse is his obtainable, decided to hold ignorance within him. But as ignorance objected to his decision, Lord Vishnu consoled ignorance and made the arrangement that during his incarnation as Rama, ignorance would overwhelm him. And because he himself accepted the curse, owing to the influence of ignorance the Rama incarnation of Vishnu has always remain forgetful about his ability during his Ramavatar.

Once, Ramachandra while living in Malyabanta Mountain was wailing in reminiscence of Sita, this was heard by a crane sitting on a Peepal tree nearby and he asked him the reason of his sorrow. Rama told everything to the crane. In conversation with the crane, Rama came to know the news about the abduction of Sita by Ravana and as the crane sympathaised with his sorrow Rama intended to bless him. The clever and idle crane asked him for making such an arrangement by which he would get food during the rainy season without going out of the nest. Ramachandra blessed him accordingly, by which he would be provided food by his wife during this period. Then when he asked that as his wife would bring food in her beak, how he would receive the orts food, Ramachandra had given advice about the pure relationship of husband and wife. Thus, in the last five days of the month of Kartika i.e. *panchuka* if non vegetarian (meat and fish) food is not taken then the fruits of the vows observed in the *Chaturmasa* (four months of rainy season) would be achieved and those five days is named as '*Bakapanchuka*' by Rama. Poet Balarama Dasa has given a number of similar such information in the Kishkindha Kanda.

Gradually the rain ceased and the autumn appeared and there was a change in the beauties and bounties of the nature. The worries of Rama increased, as there was no positive news from the side of Sugriva. In the mean time, Hanuman reminded Sugriva about the unfinished task of Rama. By the order of Sugriva, Angad and commander Nila took the responsibility of the congregation of the Vanaras (monkeys) and both of them engaged in mobilizing the Vanara warriors from all quarters. Ramachandra by being displeased on Sugriva sent Lakshmana to Kishkindha. In the mean time sage Agasti and Markanda met Rama. Lakshmana after arriving at Kishkindha sent envoy to Sugriva and the latter got afraid of him and Lakshmana was pacified by the apology of Tara. By this time, Angad entered Kishkindha with a large force of Vanaras for which Lakshmana praised him. Sugriva along with his ministers, courtiers and the great multitudes of Vanaras went to Rama and he verified and surveyed the army of the monkeys. Sugriva sent divisions of the army to the four quarters of the earth to locate Sita. Rama gave his ring and some confidential narratives about him and Sita to Hanuman to deliver to Sita when he would find her to remove her doubt about his identity. The hordes that went north, east and west returned and reported that Sita was not to be found anywhere. The eight commanders who went in the southern direction entered into a cave in their search for Sita. There they came across the recluse named Girija of Mayadaityapuri and after refreshing themselves there, they returned. The eight generals regretted their failure at Vindhyagiri. On their way, they met Sampati, the Vulture king and got the information about Sita from him. By hearing, the tale of Rama feathers began to spring and grow on his sides. The poet ended his Kishkindha Kanda by describing the story of Suparsva's preparation to take the army of Vanaras to Lanka and Angad's disagreement to that and journey of Smapati and Suparsva to the Himalayas.

Sundara Kanda

Poet Balarama Dasa invocating Lord Siva started his Sundara Kanda. Through the communication between Hara-Parvati he described the incidents following mostly the Valmiki Ramayana. He described about the assembly of the Vanaras where they were discussing about the way to transgress the sea and also measuring their ability to do so. At such a time when Hanuman expressed his readiness to go to Lanka, all had praised him. Jambavan gave many advises to Hanuman as to how he would responsibly perform his duty after reaching there.

Hanuman taking leave of the Saptasena and the army of the Vanaras bearing a huge form transgressed the sea. When he was crossing the ocean at the request of Varun devata, Mynaka, the son of Hiamlaya asked him to take rest on it and told him the story of his birth and informed him that another name of him was Maninaga. Hanuman took rest on it and Maninaga served fruits to him and gave many advises.

The Gods sent Nagamata to test the prowess of Hanuman and she came and obstructed the way of Hanuman. Both of them increased their shape and size and ultimately Nagamata was defeated and compelled to make way for Hanuman. Then poet Balarama Dasa after telling about Hanuman destroying the Rakshasi Simhika on the way and his arrival in Subalaya and described the beauty of Lanka. When the dusk approached, Hanuman decreased the size of his body and descended from the Subalaya Mountain. He entered the fortress Lanka through the northern entrance. He heard the conversation between the doorkeepers about their apprehension that a monkey like animal has entered the town in the darkness. Then he saw they closed and locked the large gates of the town. After passing a few distances, he came across the Guardian Goddess of Lanka, Lankadevi who saw him entering the town and when she tried to restrain him, Hanuman made her senseless by a strong fisticuff. Then after regaining her sense, she told Hanuman that the downfall of Lanka is imminent and the end is approaching and she transformed in to her own form and abandoned Lanka.

Hanuman in disguise searched for Sita at different places in Lanka and at last reached the palace of Ravana. He noticed the writing 'abduction of Sita-death of Ravana' on the walls of the palace. Hanuman inferred that Ravana himself indulged in this act and he abducted Sita as he wanted to die at the hands of Rama incarnation of Vishnu. Then Hanuman reached the pleasure garden of Ravana. After long description of the pleasure garden, the poet took Hanuman to the beautifully decorated innermost private apartment of Ravana. Hanuman saw there, Ravana was sleeping by taking into his lap queen Mandodari and other beautiful women doing their duties around him. He by imagining Mandodari for Sita for a moment was delighted, but in the next instant overwhelmed with sorrow and shame and cursed himself for his folly. He flew in the form of a black bee over the face of Mandodari. However, by the smell of wine coming out of the mouth of Mandodari he was assured that she was not Sita.

Hanuman went to Asokavana and found the Lakshmi like Sita sleeping under a tree. While he was waiting for an opportune moment to have a conversation with her, he saw in the last part of the night when it was still dark and not yet dawn, Ravana was approaching Asokavana. As Goddess Lanka informed Ravana in his dream about entering of spy of Rama in Lanka, he suddenly had woken up from his sleep. Thinking that the events appeared in the dream are not true, he again tried to go to sleep. But his disturbed mind increased his restiveness and he could not sleep and therefore, in the last part of night mounting on a chariot he went to Asokavana. After soliciting Sita in vain, when Ravana in anger was ready to kill Sita he was pacified by Trijata. Ravana gave the ultimatum to Sita that already ten months have passed and within two more months if Rama would not meet him, she has to become his wife. He called Rakshasis and gave them direction secretly to frighten Sita and told Trijata to make all out effort to bring about changes in her thought towards him. Ravana left Asokavana when dawn was about to approach. The sound of conch was heard in the temple. Brahma came and started reciting the Vedas and Brihaspati read the almanac.

Sita-Hanuman Coversation

After Ravana left Asokavana the Rakshasis started frightening Sita. Trijata appearing among them reprimanded them and recounted the terrible dream she had dreamt about the horripilative death of Ravana and taking of Sita by Rama from Lanka. By hearing this, they apologised Sita for their misdemeanor and the compassionate Sita forgiven them. The poet has described that Trijata, was the daughter of Vibhishana, a pious Rakshasi and she was attracted to Sita's chaste and ideal character and devoutness. The poet has described that Sita has also dreamt about a similar event. When Sita was narrating about her dream to Trijata, dawn appears and she went with Trijata for a bath in the river and the Rakshasis followed her. Hanuman hoping that now it would be possible to meet Sita privately, went to the riverside in the form of a black bee and remained hidden there in the branches of a *Sisu* (Rosewood, *Dalbergia Sisoo*) tree. When the Rakshasis left Sita alone for a while, she went near the *Sisu* tree and Hanuman saw her clearly in the day light. He was overwhelmed by her sublime beauty and divine virtue. He by forsaking his illusive form started to depict the character of Rama. Hearing the name of Rama when Sita stare up to the tree and asked who is uttering the name of Rama, Hanuman revealed himself before her. Even if he recognized Sita, he intended to ask her identity. Then Sita introduced herself and wanted Hanuman to explain who is he and the reason of wearing the crest and earring. Then Hanuman gave his identity and narrated all the events but Sita could not believe him.

In Jagamohana Ramayana unlike Valmiki Ramayana one inversion can be noticed with regard to the incident where Hanuman handed over the signet ring given to him by Rama as a sign after being questioned by Sita about any sign or memento of Rama he has with him and which she could recognize. Then Sita asked for any other information about Rama to which Hanuman described the event of '*tilak*' at Chitrakut and the story of '*Kaka*' to her. After hearing these Sita came to believe that Hanuman was a faithful and trustworthy follower of Rama. When Hanuman asked for evidence and message, which he would carry for Rama, Sita gave him the ornament worn by her on the forehead as a sign and told him the solemn promise that Rama and she had taken together by touching the lamp in the first night of the marriage as the confidential message for Rama.

Burning of Lanka

Before returning from Lanka all of a sudden evil thought struck to the mind of Hanuman and to show his prowess and strength to Ravana, he destroyed Ravana's favourite Madhuvana. The guards there were astonished to see the sudden falling of trees without any gale. By hearing, the roaring sound of Hanuman sitting on a pillar they came to know that he was the destroyer of the royal garden. When the Rakshasis asked about the monkey to Sita, she expressed her ignorance and after that, they went to Ravana's court to convey him the message. The guards also for fear of their life ran to give the bad news to Ravana. However, exactly at that time as Siva Tandav Nritya (Siva's ecstatic dance) was going on they could not get an entry to meet Ravana because of the large crowd gathered there to witness the dance. The enthusiasm of Ravana to see the Tandav Nritya and by chance, the presence of Lord Siva there on that day, Ravana expressed his desire to Brahma. Then Siva told that it would not be possible for him to dance unless Brahma would play the drum, Indra would play the cymbal, Yama would blow the trumpet, Narad play the lute, Varun play the flute and Vishnu beat time to the dance. As only Vishnu was not present in the assembly, Ravana proposed to beat time to the dance instead of Vishnu and requested Siva to perform the dance. Lord Siva could not set aside the request of his most favourite devotee, and as such wore ankle bells and started dancing. With the beginning of the dance, the earth started to tremble terribly and it moves in a circular way. Ravana fell down on the floor. By feeling his condition, frightened Ravana requested Siva to stop the dance immediately. After that, the guards and the Rakshasis conveyed to Ravana the bad news of a monkey devastating the beautiful groove. Ravana when asked to Brahma about the monkey, Brahma ordered to get hold of the monkey and bring him to the court. Ravana sent a force of eighty thousand soldiers for accomplishing this mission. After he was apprised of the news of decimation of all the soldiers, the worried Ravana again engaged many able warriors in this task. After their death, the stunned Ravana sent two hundred soldiers under the generalship of Prahasta and Jambumali. In the ensuing struggle, Jambumali died along with the soldiers and Prahasta ran away with his life. After that, he sent five generals (*Pancha Senapati*), his mighty son Akshyakumar and many able bodied commanders to the Madhuvana for accomplishing the task but in vain and all were slaughtered and put to death by Hanuman. Then the fearful Ravana sent his eldest son, the conqueror of Indra, Meghanad for capturing Hanuman. But Hanuman out of jest mirthfully reduced himself to a very small size and concealed himself among the dense trees and creepers. Meghanad, by thinking that for the fear of his presence and the soldiers, the monkey fled from there and ordered his soldiers to perform the obsequies of the dear warriors. Moreover, he declared that if anybody would find the monkey would be rewarded suitably. Though Hanuman taken shelter in the same tree under which Meghanad was resting, the demons did not find him and desisted themselves from the futile search operation. At the direction of Meghanad the rest of the trees of the royal garden were uprooted. At last, he saw Hanuman sitting on the branch of Jaiphal (*Muristica Fragrans*) tree. Hanuman had given many good advises to Meghanad. But Meghanad by an elusive war used the Nagaphasa (Serpent Dart) to capture him. By the order of Meghanad when Hanuman was taken by fifty thousand Rakshasas by holding the rope to the court of the king on foot on the highway large number of Rakshasas and Rakshasis crowded the streets to see him. Sita heard this bad news from the Rakshasis in the Asokavana. Aiming at the Asokavana she said that if Asokavana justifies the worth of its name then no sorrow would raise in her mind for Hanuman. By saying this the chaste Sita ate eight buds of Asoka tree (*Janesia Asoka*). Balarama Dasa has said probably the belief that in the bright lunar fortnight of the month of *Chaitra* if buds of Asoka tree would be taken each and everyone would be sorrow less, has been in vogue from that day. Then the moment Sita prayed to the Asokavana for the safety of Hanuman, he regained his sense and boundless strength and vigour moved in his lusterless body. Seeing Hanuman in a captive state, Indra questioned Brahma as to how Hanuman would be released. Then Brahma explained to Indra the particulars of hanuman's birth, that after his birth he unreasonable incarcerated the morning sun and as such his incarceration in future by Meghanad was made certain at that time itself by providential law and for the fulfillment of which now he was captured by Meghanad. The executioner when ready to kill Hanuman, Vibhishan protested by pointing out that the law does not permit the king to kill envoys and messengers. But Ravana did not pay heed to Vibhishana by saying that it would be a work of wisdom to kill the enemy at first chance and ordered the assailant to decapitate Hanuman by his sword. When the sword hit the thunder like body of Hanuman it was reduced to pieces and then sharp weapons like spear, axe were used to kill him but in vain. As order was given to kill him in front of the lion gate all the residents of the city made united effort to kill the monkey. As Hanuman was tied with hundred of ropes all citizens of Lanka fearlessly beaten him but he was feeling as if he was beaten with soft flowers and therefore, he had not obstructed them. At last, he pretentiously rolled on the ground and lay on the floor motionless as if he was dead. By receiving the news of his death from the executioner, Ravana ordered to bring the dead body of Hanuman to the court. At the court when someone was examining him, he got up and sat on the floor as if she was getting up from deep slumber. Indrajit was surprised to see Hanuman's regaining of life and asked Ravana how this impossible became possible. Hanuman pretentiously unfolded the secret of his death to them that he would only die by burning in fire. He told them the means that by wrapping up of rags around the tail and soaked the whole in oil and then set it ablaze and then only his death is possible. If sufficient amount of clothes would not be provided, then it would not burn and as a result, he would not die.

Hearing this, rags of all kinds were brought and wrapped round his tail. As his tail grew in size, more and more old rags were brought and were wrapped round his tail and the whole was soaked in oil and it was put on fire. Hanuman soughted pretentiously "dying dying" and suddenly shrank in size and shook off the rope that bound him. He deprecated Ravana for his foolishness for believing the enemy and intended to burn Lanka. The intense conflagration along with hurricane a number of houses and buildings were reduced to ashes. Only after Ravana warn Agni devata, the Fire God, the fire was extinguished. But as the objective was not fulfilled, Hanuman rubbed his tail on his forehead and created the fire again. As much as Ravana threatened fire, nothing had happened this time by which he was furious on Marut (the Wind God). Marut had deceived Ravana by lying him to blow Hanuman and extinguish the fire. The poet has described in details about all the regions of Lanka and depicted the ruinous picture of Lanka. At the direction of Ravana, Indra through heavy rain cooled the hot ruins of the Lanka.

Ravana was satisfied by the order of Brahma to Viswakarma to rebuild the houses of entire Lanka. Brahma met Hanuman secretly and requested him to contain the fire coming out of his forehead within him and requested him to depart immediately to Kishkindha and convey Rama of the news about Sita. At Brahma's request, Hanuman resisted the fire and requested him to make it sure that all Gods would provide security to Sita until Ramachandra arrived at Lanka. Before returning, he again met Sita and acquainted her with all the happenings occurred there. By threatening the Rakshasis to take proper care of Sita and serve her adequately, he promised Trijata to recommend Rama to deliver the reign of Lanka at the hands of her pious father, Vibhishana. He promised to bring Rama within a month to Lanka and bid farewell to Lanka. Sita blessed him for his safe and secure journey.

Return of Hanuman

After taking leave from Sita, Hanuman came to Subalaya Mountain and spent the night there. At the direction of Ravana, Indra ordered the array of clouds to extinguish the fire by heavy rain and the winds began to flow slowly. The moon appeared in the sky. In heaven, the Gods convened the assembly. Viswakarma rebuilt the fortress of Lanka by the order of Brahma. From the discussion of the Gods, it was known that twenty-four days were left for the death of Ravana. The pious Vibhishana would be the king of Lanka. Viswakarma saw, Ravana along with lakhs of young women is residing on the Puspaka Viman because of the destruction of his palace. The enraged Ravana expressed before Mandodari and other queens his idea to kill Rama and Lakshmana and teach a proper lesson to Hanuman the next morning. By hearing, this Mandodari tried to pacify Ravana. Viswakarma at this time met Ravana, told him the reason of his visit to Lanka, and presented him the Mani Akshata given by Brahma to him. He promised to rebuild Lanka before morning. By going to tell about the importance of that Mani (gems) given by Brahma, Viswakarma informed him that by wearing this jasper gem (*Chandrakanta Mani*) as a necklace all the sins and vanity would be destroyed. As and when Ravana wore the gem strung together with silk thread the sorrow of the loss of his son Akshyakumar and all other mental agonies and enervation had gone. Ravana did not understand that the Gods gave it to him as part of a conspiracy. Because the wearing of this gem would be beneficial for him as it would bring cheer and unshakableness even at the loss and destruction of property and wealth, loss of posterity, family and friends. As in the near future all his family would be extinct, probably at the loss of his posterity he might be shaken and return Sita, therefore, it was given to him to keep him free of any anxiety and keep his mind cool and calm.

Taking leave from Ravana, Viswakarma at his instruction met Meghanad. As per the direction of Viswakarma, Meghanad asked all the subjects to sleep in their own destroyed houses. After that, *Nidradevi* (Goddess of Sleep) had taken them to deep slumber. In the serenity of the night, Viswakarma started his work and before morning, he rebuilt the entire city of Lanka and made it more beautiful than before. Every paraphernalia of the houses were put in proper order so that when in the morning the citizens got up from the sleep by seeing everything they felt that the last day's events were just like a dream. In the morning, Hanuman went to the summit of the Subalaya Mountain and prepared himself for the transgression of the sea by jumping over it. The citizens of Lanka saw the huge body of Hanuman flying northwards just like a dark cloud. At that time when Ravana asked his soldiers to capture Hanuman, Vibhishana told him not to get so much excited about an ordinary monkey. Hanuman reached the other side of the ocean after seven hours.

Hanuman recounted all the happenings to the army of the monkeys, about the entire incident during his sojourn to Lanka. Then the Vanara Sena (monkey force) journeyed to Kishkindha. Hanuman went near Rama and presented him the ornament of the forehead given by Sita to him. The poet described sequentially all the events as is evident in Valmiki Ramayana but there is a personal stylistic tinge of his own in the presentation of the events.

Vibhishana's Refuge, Causeway to Lanka and Rama's entry into Lanka

When Ramachandra received the news and evidence of Sita he wailed in pangs of separation and discussed with Hanuman and Sugriva about the march to Lanka. Then in an auspicious time, Rama and Lakshmana boarding on the shoulder of Hanuman and Angad along with the large Vanara Sena marched to the seashore. Hearing the news about the arrival of Rama and Lakshmana with the soldiers on the seashore, Ravana in disbelief ordered to decapitate the spy, but Vibhishana by telling that to murder an envoy or a spy is an improper act and therefore requested him to grant freedom to the spy who brought the news. When Vibhishana presented all the incidents and events about Rama and the objective of Hanuman before Ravana, he being vexed on Vibhishana sarcastically told him to seek refuge at the feet of Rama. Even after knowing the intention of Ravana, Vibhishana advised him not to cause harm to Lanka again by such act and return Sita to Rama as soon as possible. Ravana enraged at such advice of Vibhishana, got down from his seat to slain him with his sword but Indajit restrained and pacified Ravana. Vibhishana was ordered by Ravana to leave Lanka forthwith and asked Mahi Ravana to take him outside the border of Lanka. Ravana resolved not to take dinner until Vibhishana goes out of Lanka. Vibhishana also thought it wise to leave as soon as possible and flew to the camp of Rama. In the afternoon when Sugriva and his followers were going to take bath in the sea they saw Vibhishana coming their way through the sky and were preparing to intercept him, Vibhishana gave his introduction and told them about his purpose of coming there. Then at the instance of Sugriva his followers took Vibhishana near Rama. Sugriva mistrusted the good faith of Vibhishana because he was of the opinion that Rakshasas are adepts in duplicity. Having thus expressed his feelings, Sugriva awaited Rama's reply. Rama heard patiently the various views of the Vanara chiefs and found satisfaction in Hanuman's utterance who spoke for Vibhishana and Trijata. Thus, Rama ordered Sugriva to give him a cordial reception and bring him with all hospitality. When Lakshmana doubted the intentions of Vibhishana, the latter taking various oaths and swearings expressed his desire to take sanctuary at the feet of Rama. Then Lakshmana approached Rama and told about the swearing of Vibhishana. Rama explained to Lakshmana about the inherent meanings of Vibhishana's request and removed his suspicions. He also told Lakshmana about the anticipatory situation going to happen in the upcoming *Kaliyuga*. Then Vibhishana was allowed to meet Rama and lo and behold, Vibhishana by seeing the Rama incarnation of Vishnu purified his eyes. He after praying Rama told him about Lanka and about the wealth and riches of Ravana. After Vibhishana took refuge, Rama promised him the kingship of Lanka and coroneted him there in his camp and made him his minister.

Ramachandra asked Sugriva about the means, which can be adopted to cross the sea. Sugriva told him that it would be proper to please Varun and work under his direction to which Jambavan also supported. Ramachandra prayed Varun and when the latter did not appear, he picketed there sitting on Darbha grass spread.

Meanwhile when Ravana got the news from Indrajit and Mahi Ravana that Vibhishana had taken refuge near Rama and he deputed spies to keep a watch on his movements. When the spy reported the whole matter and happenings in the camp of Rama, Ravana became worried. He again deputed his trusted lieutenants, Suka and Sarana to the camp of Rama to reconnoiter the military prowess, preparations and arrangements of Rama, to bring Vibhishana back by convincing him, to seduce Sugriva to switch over to their side by telling him that Ravana was once an intimate friend of his brother Vali. Vibhishana strongly denied their offer and told them to return to Lanka. When Sugriva rebuked and resiliently reproached the Rakshasa spies the Vanaras caught hold of them and manhandled them and Angad even thrashed them. Then Balarama Dasa described that when Rama received no response from the God of the Sea, to break his arrogance he took up his bow, put his arrow on it intending to dry up the infinitude of waters of the seven seas making them bereft of all life, Varuna along with Ganga and Yamuna could stand it no longer appeared before Rama and prayed him for mercy. Varuna advised Rama to build a causeway with the help of Nala and he also informed Rama that because of the blessing of sages, the stone can float on the water by the touch of the hands of Nala. Thus, started the construction of the causeway under the surveillance and leadership of Nala. After the causeway was ready, Hanuman and Angad put sands on it for making it convenient for movement. The poet described the episode of how a squirrel put sands on the bridge as per his ability and Rama adored the squirrel for his concern and effort. Rama worshipped Sivalinga of Ramesvaram and along with his army started his march to Lanka in an auspicious time. They reached the foothills of the Subalaya Mountain of Lanka.

Lankakanda

Balarama Dasa after a long prayer of Lord Jagannath through Hara-Parvati conversation began the description of Lanka Kanda.

Ravana was worried by hearing the news of the march of Rama with his force. Here the poet has mentioned about *Sardula* (Tiger). The Sardula did not enter inside the forces of Rama and by the power of the spell given to him by Narada put collyrium in his eyes climbed up the ramparts of the fortress of Lanka and sitting on it comprehended the forces of Rama. Not only the forces near Subalaya, he through his long-sightedness got by the power of the spell, was able to see the presence of the Vanara force of Rama throughout the *Jambudvipa* (the Island of Jambu).

Then the poet dealt in detail with the events from the protection of the fortress of Lanka to the seize of Lanka. Ravana sent off the Gods from Lanka for fear of activities of spies of the enemy side. By seeing Rama dressed as a soldier and warrior the Gods worshipped him. Meanwhile Ravana tried to mollify and beguile Sita by showing her the deceptive severed head of Rama in the Asokavana and Sita was pained to see that but she did not believe the *mayavi* Ravana. She told to Trijata as the sages predicted, there is no sign of any widowhood in her life. Through their conversation, the poet described in detail the nature of various type of womanhood.

After returning from Asokavana, Ravana saw the Vanaras are moving fearlessly on the northern entrance of the city and he ordered his soldiers to start the war. Large number of soldiers died from both sides. Then when he himself was surveying the army of Rama, he threw the mace towards Rama and in turn, Rama captured the mace and shot his arrow cutting through his one lakh umbrella. At this, Ravana felt ashamed and escaped to Lanka. Then Rama deputed Angad as his envoy to the court of Ravana. Angad went to the court of Ravana and prepared a seat for himself by coiling his tail in his court and sitting on it conveyed the message of Rama. Depicting the valour of Rama, Angad advised Ravana to return Sita gracefully. The enraged Ravana ordered one hundred Rakshasas to kill him but Angad increased the size of his body and caught hold of the hair of five hundred Rakshasas on either side of him and killed them brutally. When he leaped out of the assembly he had broken off the beautiful tower decorated with gems. The demons present there were stunned and filled with fear by such display of prowess by Angad. He returned and explained all the events to Rama in detail.

Nagaphasa (Serpent Darts)

There was an intense fight between the army of both sides. Hanuman fought with Indrajit. When there was sunset, the war was stopped at the direction of Rama. After evening prayer, Rama discussed with the commanders of the Vanara Sena, the plan of action of the war for the next day. Ravana was frightened at the death of his commanders and thought about the next day's war. Poet Balarama Dasa has described in sequence the incidents such as- departure of Hanuman to Lanka with the message from Rama, the war between Rama and Ravana, Ikshavaku's unconsciousness by the blow of Shakti by Indrajit, the vow of Lakshmana to kill Indrajit, the description of war by Ravana and his praise of the heroism of Rama-Lakshmana,

Indrajit's anger over Ravana's praise of the enemy, the swooning of the Vanara Sena by the deceptive war of Indrajit etc. Then the poet went on to describe that Ravana being informed about the condition of Rama and Lakshmana by the spies, his praise of Indrajit, order of Ravana to Trijata to take Sita in the *Puspakayana* to see the condition of Rama and Lakshmana, Sita's visit to the battlefield and her bewailing by seeing Rama and Lakshmana motionless, Trijata's consolation to Sita, the discussion of the army of the Vanaras for the release of Rama and Lakshmana, Rama's remembrance of Garuda and Garuda's visit and the subsequent release of Rama and Lakshmana from the Nagaphasa.

Killing of Kumbhakarna

Balarama Dasa followed Valmiki Ramayana in narrating the Kumbhakarna episode. Some difference can be noticed as he mentioned that when Vibhishana was telling about Kumbhakarna, Ravana and Kumbhakarna both visited a place of pilgrimage in Odisha, which was famous as Biraja and engaged in penances here. Balarama Dasa has also mentioned that Kumbhakarna woke up from sleep once in a year. Kumbhakarna was frightened when he came to know that the powerful Vali was killed by Rama. In the duel with Kumbhakarna, Ramachandra ultimately killed him by severing his head.

Killing of Meghanad

Indrajit had fought several times with Rama's army. One of the fights has been mentioned in the aforesaid discussion. In the second battle, Indrajit consoled the sorrowful father and vowed to avenge the death of his brothers. Before going to the battlefield, he performed *yajna* under a Peepal tree and mounted on a chariot named '*Devadalana*' given by Agni marched ahead. When he shot the Brahmastra to destroy Rama and Lakshmana along with the Vanara Sena at once in that very moment for their safety all the gods sent Pavan Devata (Wind God) near Rama. Pavan had advised Rama to pray the *astra* and Rama identifying himself as the lord of the unending crores of Universe prayed the *brahmastra*. Because of that, the Brahmastra did not take their life but only made them unconscious. Indrajit by considering that all of them are dead proceeded to sever their head. During that moment at the request of the Gods, Goddess Saraswati, the Goddess of speech and eloquence resided in his heart. As a result of which the thought that it would not be a heroic deed to sever the head of a dead person and if done would be an act of deprecation, comes to the mind of Indrajit and he restrained himself from doing such an inimical act. Coming out of Subalaya camp when Vibhishana saw the bodies of Rama and Lakshmana and the entire army lying in a dead like condition he bewailed and approached Hanuman first and tried to bring him back to consciousness. After Hanuman regaining his consciousness, both of them went to Jambavan for his advice and discuss with him the next course of action. By the effort of both of them Jambavan regained his consciousness and advised Hanuman to bring medicine from Gandhamardan Mountain as soon as possible. Hanuman being unable to recognize the exact medicine brought the entire mountain to Lanka. Susena and Jambavan both had taken the medicinal plants from different parts of the mountain and by utilizing those, they recuperated Rama, Lakshmana and the Vanaras.

The last war with Indrajit was not fought in the battlefield but in the sacrificial place in the Nikumbhila Mountain. The poet described about the incident of illusory Site here. Indrajit ordered the son of Jambumali, Singhanada to create an illusory Sita. As such, Singhanada along with his widowed sister Sukanti went to the place of pilgrimage of Triveni. Sukanti by jumping into the calm water of Triveni with the illusory power of Singhanada obtained the form of Sita. Indrajit took her to the battlefield and killed her there. Rama became woeful by hearing the news of assassination of Sita. At this moment a Rakshasi, named Nikula met Vibhishana in the form of a monkey delivered the news about the tactics of Indrajit and Vibhishana consoled Rama by telling him that the murdered Sita was an illusory Sita conceptualized by Indrajit. Thence, Vibhishana told the secrecy of the death of Indrajit. Lakshmana, the Vanara Sena along with Vibhishana marched to the Nikumbila. At that time, Indrajit was performing a *yajna*, which was interrupted and destroyed by them. When Vibhishana advised Lakshamana about the mode of operation, Indrajit reproached him for that. At last, Lakshmana killed Indrajit with the help of the Gods.

Death of Ravana

The poet depicted that to avenge the death of his son, Ravana engaged in intense fighting. When he shot the Ekaghni Brahmastra built by Brahma himself towards the murderer of his son and the conspirator who took Lakshmana to Nikimbhila, the disgrace of Lanka, Vibhishana, Lakshmana came in front of him suddenly and in turn was grievously injured and fell down by the blow of that *astra*. By seeing Lakshmana lying in a dead like condition, Rama was tormented with grief. Susena consoled Rama and sent Hanuman to Gandhamardan Mountain to bring medicine. The poet described the journey of Hanuman to Gandhamardan, his encounter with Kalanemi, his fight with the Gandharvas, his meeting with Bharata at the time of bringing the mountain on his head and his entering into Lanka with medicinal mountain etc.

After the death of the son and the last commander, Veerabahu having no other option, Ravana decided to go to the battlefield himself. At the time of conversation with Mandodari, he told her about his past life and also the event of his previous birth. Mandodari also told about the tale of Rama and Sita as told to her by Devarshi Narada. As Rama is Vishnu himself and Sita is Lakshmi, she requested Ravana not to continue enmity with them and surrender Sita to Rama and save his life. Ravana also told her that despite being aware of Rama and Sita's identity he is doing all this because of his emancipation. He tried to console Mandodari by telling about his previous birth, his severe penance, the blessing of Brahma and the reason of his death and the possibility of his death only by the Brahmastra etc.

Ravana ordering his ministers to remain prepare for the war went to the harem. There he discussed about his upcoming fight with his queens. All the queens requested him to return Sita but he defied them by telling them about his various resolves to destroy his enemies. Ravana before his march to the battlefield went to the Asokavana to meet Sita for the last time. He expressed his inner feeling before Sita and as before made obscene comments about her beauty and adolescence and at the same time repeated his resolve to kill Rama and Lakshmana in the battle next day. Sita reproached Ravana for this. The poet mentions that in the night both Ravana and Mandodari had a bad dream. In the morning, Ravana along with all of his remaining soldiers and commanders marched to the battlefield.

By hearing Ravana coming to the war, Rama also prepared himself for the war. Ravana displayed his excellent military strategy by forming many military orders in the war. Both sides engaged in tumultuous fight. Ravana praised the display of great military prowess by Rama. All the Gods and Goddesses for the convenience of Rama sent the chariot with the flag of Garuda along with the charioteer Matali. At the request of the Gods, Nandikesvar resided in a hidden manner on the wheel of the chariot and created enormous sound. For that matter, the poet has given a new name to the chariot, 'Nandighosa'. The Gods also sent for Rama the Matula, the imperishable quiver and many weapons. Ravana, by seeing Rama with Matali on the Nandighosa chariot, firmly ascertained that Rama is none other than Vishnu himself and a wave of fear spread in his heart. He was frightened to see the gigantic figure of Rama. Still then, he did not abandon the duty of a warrior and continued his fight. By seeing Ravana losing his vigour Vibhishana also shot arrows towards him and when Ravana became senseless by the blow of his arrows, the charioteer considering Ravana as dead took his chariot to a safer place. After a few moments when Ravana regained consciousness, he reproached the charioteer and ordered him to march towards the battlefield. Despite fighting incessantly, Rama did not succeed in killing Ravana. Rama was surprised and baffled to see the growing of the heads of Ravana often cut off before repeatedly. When he asked Matali about the reason of this, Matali disclosed the secret of his invincibility to Rama. Thence, Rama took out the Brahmastra given by sage Agasti from his quiver. By seeing the Brahmastra in the hand of Rama, Ravana became aware that his death is inevitable at the hands of Rama. At the last moment, he shots hundreds and thousands of arrows and mangled Matali, Rama, Lakshaman, Vibhishana and prominent commanders and warriors of Vanara Sena. When Rama by praying and uttering spells shot the Brahmastra, all the arrows of Ravana became futile. The Brahmastra pierced through his bosom and came out from his back and Ravana groaningly toppled on the ground. After destroying Ravana by the Brahmastra, the whole world appeared as dark to Rama and he lost his eyesight. He asked the reason of this to Matali and the latter told him it is due to the crime of slaying a Brahmin and he advised Rama to remember and utter his own name. Rama through the process of yoga remembered the *Ramataraka Mantra* and consumed his sins and regained his eyesight. By depicting such incidents, Balarama Dasa tried to give prominence to the concept of *nama mahatmya* i.e. the importance of the worship of the name of Almighty.

Sita's Agnipariksha(Fire Ordeal of Sita)

After the coronation of Vibhishana, Rama through Hanuman sent the news of his victory over Ravana to Sita. By hearing from Hanuman that Sita was anxious to meet him, Ramachandra ordered Vibhishana to make necessary arrangements to bring Sita. When Sita was coming to meet Rama on a palanquin, by seeing the guards of Vibhishana were manhandling the concourse of Vanaras by pushing them aside who were anxiously waiting to have a view of Sita, Rama became angry and ordered Vibhishana to make sure that no one be pushed away and make proper arrangements for Sita to come on foot through the Vanara Sena. As per the order of Rama

Sita came on foot following Vibhishana and stood besides Rama. He told Sita that, "I retributed the insult of the enemy. I have doubt about the chastity of your character. One's own wife after living so long in a stranger's house no husband would accept her again. I have no attraction towards you anymore. Now you may go wherever you want." By hearing such bitter words from Rama, Sita swear by her chastity. Even then, as Rama did not accept her, he entered into the flames kindled by Lakshamana. The Gods had presented a number of arguments with regard to the clean character of Sita and prayed Rama not to take such a harsh decision. At last, Agni, the God of Fire rose in his own form out of the flame, lifted her and presented her to Rama and provided the evidence of the chastity of Sita. He requested Rama to accept her without any doubt. Rama put forward the justification of his decision to examine Sita in such a way to the Gods.

Return of Rama to Ayodhaya

After the fire ordeal of Sita, Vibhishana requested Rama to dress up in royal attire but Rama disagreed to his suggestion. Then he discussed with Vibhishana about the preparation for his return to Ayodhya. Vibhishana introduced the Puspakayana (Aerial Chariot) to Rama and the latter worshipped the vehicle. However, Rama sent Hanuman to Srungaverpur and Nandigram with the news of his return in order to know the feelings and reaction of Bharata and the ministers. When Rama did not return on time and Bharata was expressing his sorrow for this near Vashistha, Hanuman heard the whole conversation by remaining in the sky. In the mean time, Rama sent Angad to Guhyak to tell him to go to Ayodhya. Rama introduced Vibhishana, the Vanaras and others to Bharata who gave them due respect. After entering Ayodhya, Rama travelled throughout the town. Rama went again to Nandigrama and discussed with Vashistha about the ascertainment of the auspicious day for his coronation. All the materials for the occasion were collected and all the sages were invited to Ayodhya and the coronation took place. After coronation, adoration of Rama and Sita took place in the harem and the Gods presented various gifts to Rama.

The poet has compared the Puspakayatra of Rama with the *Gundichayatra* (Car Festival) of Lord Jagannath in the second day of lunar fortnight of the month of Asadha. At the time of returning on the Puspakayana the poet described the places of Nilagiri, Konark, Ekamrakanan etc. along with other places. He several times compared Rama's *Rathyatra* with the *Rathyatra*

(Car Festival) of Lord Jagannath. Likewise, the poet compared the ablution and purification ceremony of Rama and Sita during the coronation ceremony with the *Snanayatra* (Ablution ceremony) of Lord Jagannath of Srikhetra. This proves the poet's inner love and devotion towards Lord Jagannath.

Uttara Kanda

Abandonment of Sita

Rama's abandonment of Sita has been discussed by Balarama where he mentioned the two extant reasons such as public infamy and the curse of Tara, wife of Vali for the abandonment. Despite that, the poet attributed another vicarious reason created from his own conception that *devatas* (Gods) in the heaven were worried about the return of Vishnu incarnation of Rama to Vaikuntha, the eternal abode of Lord Vishnu. They were happy to learn from Brahma about the return of Rama to Vaikuntha soon by renouncing Ayodhya. The poet's invocation of Janaki, description of the nature in the six seasons during the roaming of Rama and Sita in the jungle, the praise of Rama by Bharata, Rama's description of the signs of Sita's pregnancy, the donations of Sita to the indigent Brahmins have a typical touch of his own style.

Meanwhile Rama talked about his intention with Bharata to perform a *yajna*. Bharata advised Rama to perform *Aswamedha Yajna* instead of *Rajasuya Yajna*. Vashistha approved the proposal of Bharata and informed Rama about the importance of *Aswamedha Yajna*. At the instance of Rama, Lakshmana went to invite the courtiers, friends and relatives and sages. Ramachandra prepared the place of *yajna* in the forest of Naimisa situated at the bank of river Gomati. By worshipping the horse of *yajna*, tying victory flag on the head of the horse he had given the responsibility to Lakshmana to perambulate the sacrificial horse around the world in due time. Sita heard about the *Aswamedha Yajna* from sage Valmiki and she at the request of Valmiki agreed to send her two sons to the place of *yajna*. Ramachandra after getting the identity of Lava and Kusha accepted them with great love and fondness. At the request of the kings and sages Ramachandra sent Bharata, Lakshmana, Satrughna, Sugriva, Vibhishana, Hanuman and Angada with Valmiki for bringing back Sita. Even if Rama said "I have no fear for peoples' reproach", even if Valmiki swear by the blamelessness of Sita, even if Rama praise Sita in public that pure this body is by trial and ordeal" (*parikshita e tanu atai punyarasi*), he requested Sita to submit an ordeal again for the knowledge of the subjects of Ayodhya. Sita by going to prove her chastity by ordeal appealed to the earth to split into two parts to which the earth obliged unhesitatingly and appeared immediately and with a great deal of praise for Sita took her daughter into her lap by extending her hands. And thus, Sita entered the nether world.

The poet has described that after entering the nether world Sita obtained the form of Lakshmi and went to Vaikuntha. The poet mentioned that her effort precipitated the ascension of Ramachandra to heaven. He discussed lengthily the various aspects of events like –the sorrow of Rama for delivering death sentence to Lakshmana, Rama being consoled by Bharata and Vashistha, the lamentation of the subjects of Ayodhya for the abandonment of Lakshmana, Lakshmana's penance in the forest and Indra and other God's invocation of Lakshmana, taking of the celestial form by Lakshmana and returning to Vaikuntha and his conversation with Saraswati, the mental agony of Rama reminiscing Lakshmana and Sita, the invocation of Rama by Brahma along with other Gods, Rama taking the form of Vishnu with four arms (*Chaturbhuja*), Bharata's taking the form of *Chakra* and Satrughna taking the form of *Sankha*, the welcoming of Vishnu incarnate Rama by the Gods of heaven, return of all the Vanaras, demons, the inhabitants of Ayodhya, after taking bath in river Sarayu to heaven in celestial forms by the direction of Brahma, entering of Vishnu in Vaikuntha and his union with Lakshmi etc. Balarama Dasa in a way made his presentation rich and voluminous which obviously display his poetic ability.

THE EPILOGUE

Like the thematic aspects, the characters are one of the prime bases of any great epic. The epic transforms into a beautiful form with the combination of both well-defined storyline and an equally well-conceptualized and calibrated characterisation. As there is a cleavage of time between the Valmiki Ramayana and the vernacular Ramayanas of later periods it is but natural that there would be an imprint of the changing time and circumstances, of ideal and ideologies, of customs and tradition on the style of presentation of the themes. As a skillful poet Balarama Dasa was a keen observer of the society and social life of the contemporaneous time, he keenly studied the human nature and therefore was able to provide a real and lively form to his characters in the epic.

In the annals of Indian history, social condition has largely been reflected in the literatures of the various periods. As literature is the mirror of the society, it reflects in it the basic fundamental aspects of society be it customs, traditions and heritages of different periods. Litterateurs gets ample opportunities for the manifestation and germination of their ideal, thoughts, creativities which are germane to the social practices in the literatures of their times Moreover the literatures over the passage of time have found a niche among the historical sources as an important material used for the construction of history. As poetries and epics were written on the background of the social life, it is quite natural that the contemporary social picture is reflected in Ramayana.

In the Jagamohana Ramayana, Balarama Dasa had presented similarly the contemporary social picture and tradition, which was basically a flow of Hinduism and at places there is a reflection of localization. The existence and practice of Varnashrama Dharma can be found in it. Much importance was given to the Brahmins as they were given the highest place in the social structure. He had written at a number of places where he repeatedly stressed on donation to them munificently and show sufficient devotion and respect to them. It has also been found that if the Brahmins would not be able to perform their duties, they were deprecated and reproached by the poet. He even went to the extent of terming them as most vicious than others. This type of Brahmins without performing evening prayers , uttering the *Gayatri mantra*, doing *Agnipuja*, prayer of Vasudeva were only interested in donations and sacrificial fees. He mentioned that because of these traits and temperament they were reproached and cursed by Ramachandra at the pilgrimages. Therefore, he did not hesitate and refrained from openly criticizing the exploiting and avaricious tendency of the Brahmins and also vociferously protested such activities of theirs. Through the example of the conflict between Viswamitra and Vashistha he opined that anybody can become a Brahmin by dint of his perseverance.

There is reference of a number of castes in his Ramayana like, Teli, Tanti, Mali, Kumbhar, Gudia etc. but emphasis has been given by him about the duties and activities of Brahmins and the Kshatriyas who were entitled to rule. Regarding the role of an ideal Kshatriya he repeatedly mentioned at many places like- the query of sage Rusyasrunga to king Lomapada and Dasaratha about the duties of a king, similar questions of sage Viswamitra to Dasaratha, the advises of Dasaratha to Rama regarding the duties of Kshatriyas before coronation of the latter and the question of sage Agasti to Rama etc.

Regarding the position of women in the society from his Ramayana it is known that generally the women are provided high place in the social system as a wife and a mother. It is evident that from Manusmriti to different other works women were accorded high and respectable positions in the family and society. In the Ramayana there are depictions of different categories of women with their defined works and activities. There is mention of two types of women folk i.e. *ganika* (prostitute) and virtuous wife. The name of Jarata and Kamamohini has been mentioned as *ganikas* and though the necessity of these *ganikas* in performing dances in various auspicious occasion had been felt but it cannot be found anywhere that they had any type of honourable position in the society. In his Ramyana, wife and virtuous woman has acquired a special status in the society. There is the reference of polygamy as it has been mentioned that Dasaratha had seven hundred and fifty queens. Balarama Dasa mentioned Ravana had around three crore wives.

The poet by way of conversation between Ravana and the Angel has mentioned the different meaning of the names ascribed to women as such- Pramada as she creates amusement and delight in man, Vama as she evokes thoughtfulness in the mind, Vallabhi as she evokes delight, joy and affection in life, Yuvati as she fascinated the young, Kutumba as she creates family, Angana as she bears beauty in her body, Saubhagi as man becomes fortunate by getting her, Dharmapatni as with her cooperation religious ceremonies are accomplished etc. Not only that the Angel had honoured the woman as the first mother and the creator of the whole creation.

Thus, the Angel's opinion was that in the whole world the position of woman is most important. The creator has created women after eating the best of the food. On the lips she bears the nectar, on the face she bears the moon, in the eyes she bears the five arrows of the cupid (*panchavana*). Her youth is like sweet fruits. Life is meaningful and successful in her lap only. From all sides women is full of glory.

The poet at the same time has also described the fault and the bad quality of women. After exiling Sita to the forest when Lakshmana returned, he consoled the worried Rama by telling him that how woman is at the root of all problems.

Despite this, the poet in Jagamohana Ramayana has always depicted the picture of man and woman's ideal matrimonial life, and the woman in the role of a virtuous wife. He depicted woman as a tolerant, chaste, faithful, devoted and responsible wife. In the Ramayana not only Sita but also Kausalya, Sumitra, Tara, Mandodari, Sarama and the wives of the sages have not been deficient of such qualities.

A necroscopic analysis can bring to fore the reflection of fifteenth and sixteenth century's socio-political and cultural picture of Odisha in his Ramayana. The family life of Utkala (Odisha), its idealism, life of a house holder, societal rules and regulations, different types of human behavioural practices, the royal duties, administrative rules and regulations, relation between king and subjects, the moral and ethical ideals extant in the society, devotional feelings, religious currents, duties and activities of different communities, conduct and misconduct, food and drinks, dressings, social customs, amusements, military practices, the role of women in the society and the depiction of hamlets etc. have been recorded. The magnanimity and dexterity of the poet can be judged from the quality of comprehensiveness and compactness inherent in his narratives. His attempts in the Jagamohana Ramayana is a rare combination of his imagery and pragmatism and his ability to conglomerate different elements of his thoughts within the ambit of the theme of his epic.

BIBLIOGRAPHY

ODIA

Jagamohan Ramayan (1st and 2nd Edition)	:	a). Nityananda Pustakalaya, Balu Bazar, Cuttack b). Dharmagrantha Store, Cuttack
Acharya Brundaban	:	Odia Sahityara Sankshipta Parichya, Grantha Mandir, Cuttack, 1977
Das, Nilakantha	:	Odia Sahityara Kramaparinama (1st, 2nd, and 3rd Part), New Students Store, Cuttack, 1977
Das, Suryanarayan	:	Odia Sahityara Itihas, Part-I, Grantha Mandir, Cuttack, 1978
Das, Chittaranjan	:	Achyutananda and Panchsakha Dharma, Odisha Rajya Pathya Pustaka Pranayan O Prakasan Sanstha, Bhubaneswar, 1981
Panda, Bhagaban	:	Odishara Dharma, Grantha Mandir, Cuttack, 1979
Panigrahi, Krushna Chandra	:	Prabandha Manas, Kitab Mahal, Cuttack, 1972
Mohanty, Debendra	:	Panchasakha O Odia Sahitya, Friends Publisher, Cuttack, 1973
Mohanty Bansidhar	:	Odia Sahityara Itihas, Friends Publisher, Cuttack, 1977
Mohanty, Surendra	:	Odia Sahityara Madhya Parva, Cuttack Students Store, Cuttack, 1979
______________	:	Odia Sahityara Kramavikas, Agraduta, Cuttack, 1978
Manasingha, Mayadhar	:	Odia Sahityara Itihas, Grantha Mandir, Cuttack, 1967
Mishra, Kanhu Charan	:	Odia Sahityre Dharmadhara, Friends Publisher, Cuttack, 1978
Rajguru, Syamasundar	:	Prabandhabali, Odisha Sahitya Academi, 1917
Samantaray, Natabar	:	Sakhahina Panchasakha, Vani Bhavan, Samantarapur, Bhubaneswar, 1975
Sahu, Krushna Charan	:	Prachin Sahitya, Janashakti Pustakalaya, Cuttack, 1982
Sahu, Navin Kumar	:	Odia Jatira Itihas, Odisha Rajya Pustaka Pranayan O Prakasan Sanstha, Bhubaneswar, 1977

ENGLISH

Agarwal, V. S. : India as known to Panini, Lucknow University (Publisher), 1953

Basham, A.L. : Wonder That Was India, 1969

Bath, A : Religions of India: Authorised Trans by Rev. J. Wood, Chowkhamba Sanskrit Series, Varanasi, 1963

Bhandarkar, R. C. : Vaishnivism, Saivisim and other minor religious systems, Indological Book Houses, Varanasi, 1965

Das, A. C. : Rig Vedic India, Vol. I, Calcutta, 1921

Das, C. : Studies in Medieval Religion and Literatures of Orissa, Biswa Bharati Studies-14, Santiniketan, 1951

Das, D. N. : The Early History of Kalinga, Punthi Pustak, Calcutta, 1977

Das, M. N. (Ed) : Sidelights on History and Culture of Orissa, Vidyapuri, Cuttack, 1977

Dasgupta, S. N. and De, S. K.: History of Sanskrit Literature, Vol-I, Calcutta, 1962

Farquhar, J. N. : An Outline of Religious Literature in India, Oxford, 1920

Gonda, J. : Aspects of Early Vishnuism, Motilal Banarasidas, Delhi, 1969

Haque, M.A. : Muslim Administration in Orissa (1568-1751), Punthi Pustak, Calcutta, 1980

Hopkins, E.W. : The Religions of India, Munshiram Manoharlal, New Delhi, 1970

Jolly, J. : The Institutes of Vishnu, [Trans. By Julius Jolly, Sacred Book of the East, Ed. By F. Max Muller, Vol., VIII, Motilal Banarasidass, Delhi, 1970

Kane, P. V, : History of Dharmasastra, Vol. II, Poona, 1941

Keith, A. B. : History of Sanskrit Drama, Oxford, 1924

Majumdar, B.C. : Typical Selections from Oriya Literature, Part-I, Published by C.U., 1921

Majumdar, R. C. : Vedic Age, Bharatiya Vidya Bhavan, Bombay, 1965

__________ : Ancient India, Motilal Banarsidass, Delhi, 1987

Manasingh, M. : History of Oriya Literature, Sahitya Academy, New Delhi, 1962

Mani, Vettam : Puranic Encyclopaedia, Motilal Banarsidass, Delhi, 2015

Max Muller, F. : Lectures on the Origin and Growth of Religion, Indological Book House, Varanasi, 1964

Mehta, P. D. : Early Indian Religious Thoughts, Luzac & Co. Ltd.,

London, 1956

Sahoo, K. C. : Literature and Social Life Medieval Orissa, Pustak Sadan, Ranchi, 1971

Sahu, N. K. and Others : History of Orissa, Nalanda, Cuttack, 1979

Sarkar Jadunath : India Through The Ages, Disha Books (Orient Longman), New Delhi, 1993

Sastri Nilakanta, K.A. : Aryan and Dravidian, Sachi Publication, Ajmer, 1979

Srivastav, A. L. : Medieval Indian Culture, Shivlal Agrawal & Co., Agra, 1971

Thapar Romila et al : India: Historical Beginning and the Concept of the Aryan, NBT, India, 2007

Varadachari, K. C. : Alvars of South India, Bharatiya Vidya Bhavan, Bombay, 1906

Weber, A. : On the Ramayan, English Translation by D.C. Boyd, Bombay, 1873

Appendix I

GLOSSARY

Agneyastra	:	A missile charged with an invocation to the God Agni (Fire)
Ashrama	:	Hermitage
Astras	:	Miraculous weapons whose power lay in the invocation they were charged with
Avatar	:	Incarnation
Bhagarathi	:	Another of Ganga
Bhakta	:	Devotee
Bhakti	:	Devotion to God, loyalty, faith
Brahmana	:	The first of the four castes devoting their lives to study and teaching and the performance of religious ceremonies
Brahma	:	The Creator, one of the Trinity
Brahmastra	:	The most powerful among astras
Brahmachari	:	One who is in the first of the four stages in Brahmin's life, the stage of study and practice of a disciplined life
Brahmajnana	:	The realization of Supreme Being, higher wisdom
Brahmarishi	:	The highest type of sages
Brihaspati	:	The preceptor of the Devas
Chaitra	:	The month falling in the second half of April and the first half of May
Chandala	:	Outcaste, untouchable
Dana	:	Gift
Danavas	:	Enemies of Devas
Darbha	:	A species of sacred grass used for religious rites
Deva-Loka	:	The celestial regions
Devarishis	:	Sages of Heavens
Devas	:	Celestial beings, sons of Aditi and Kasyapa
Dharma	:	Duty as laid down by religion or custom
Gandharvas	:	A Class of semi-divine beings
Garuda	:	The bird king who is Vishnu's vehicle
Govinda	:	One of the names of Krishna
Guru	:	Acharya, preceptor
Hari	:	One of the names of Vishnu
Himavan	:	The presiding deity of the Himalaya range
Ikshvaku	:	King of the Solar race from whom the name came for the race of Solar Kings
Indra	:	The chief and the king of the Gods
Jambavan	:	Leader of bears in the army of Sugriva

Jambudvipa	:	One of the Puranically famous Saptadvipas (seven continents). These seven continents are embankments separating the seven seas.
Jnana	:	Spiritual knowledge, realization
Jnani	:	A knower of Reality
Kama	:	Desire, usually referred to in relation to sex
Kamadhenu	:	The Divine cow of Heaven. It was born of the Ocean when the Devas and Asuras churned it for Nectar
Kailasa	:	The abode of Siva
Karma	:	Action, the law that governs all action and its inevitable consequences on the doer
Kasyapa	:	A celebrated sage, son of Brahma. He had many wives through whom were born the various forms of life on earth
Kshatriya	:	The second of the four castes
Kubera	:	God of Wealth
Kusa	:	A kind of grass used in religious ceremonies
Lakshmi	:	The Goddess of well-being
Maruti	:	Name of Hanuman being son of Marut, the Wind-God
Mahadeva	:	One of the names of Siva
Maharshi	:	A great Sage
Mantras	:	Scriptural verses, incantations
Maya	:	The architect of Asuras
Naga	:	Semi-divine serpents
Narayana	:	Vishnu
Narada	:	The celestial rishi with the lute
Nandigrama	:	A village near Ayodhya where Bharata lived and ruled Ayodhya as deputy of Rama
Nikumbhila	:	A cave and grove in Lanka where oblations were offered to Kali
Parvati	:	Uma, wife of Siva
Parasurama	:	The sixth incarnation of Vishnu who curbed the growing arrogance of the Kshatriyas
Puja	:	Worship
Prajapati	:	The Creator
Puranas	:	Sacred legends
Puspaka-Vimana	:	Aerial chariot of Ravana which originally belonged to Kubera
Rakshasas	:	Evil-minded strong beings
Rakshasis	:	Feminine of Rakshasa
Raghu	:	An ancestor of Rama. He was a king of the Solar race
Rishi	:	A sage who has undergone severe austerities
Rudra	:	Siva

Sastras	:	Sacred lore
Sarama	:	Wife of Vibhishana
Sarayu	:	A tributary of the river Ganges on the North bank
Siva	:	One of the Hindu Trinity
Sloka	:	Couplet or Quatrain in Sanskrit
Surya	:	The Sun God
Sri Krishna	:	The eighth incarnation of Vishnu, who gave the Bhagavad Gita
Sruti	:	Veda, Revelation
Sukra	:	The Guru of the Asuras, the Planet Venus
Swarga	:	Heaven
Tapasya	:	Power obtained through penance
Vanaprashtha	:	The third stage of a Brahmin's life retiring with his wife as a preparation for sanyasa
Vayu	:	The Wind God who was father of Hanuman
Vaishnava	:	Appertaining to Vishnu or worship of Vishnu
Varuna	:	The Lord of the Ocean
Veda	:	Scripture. Four books-Rig Veda, Yajur Veda, Sama Veda and Atharva Veda
Viswakarma	:	The celestial architect
Yajna	:	Sacrifice, a religious ceremony accomplished by oblations
Yama	:	God of Death
Yojana	:	A measure of distance equal probably to nine miles

Appendix II

VARIOUS DIVYASTRAS

A Divyastras is a missile charged with power by holy incantation. After killing Tataka, Visvamitra reveals to Rama and Lakshmana the secret of using a great many varieties of Divyastras* some of those are:

1. Dandacakra
2. Dharmacakra
3. Kalacakra
4. Vishnucakra
5. Indracakra
6. Vajrastra
7. Saivasula
8. Aisika
9. Brahmasirastra
10. Brahmastra
11. Modakisikhari
12. Dharmapasa
13. Kalapasa
14. Varunastra
15. Varunapasa
16. Paramastra
17. Pinakastra
18. Narayanastra
19. Agneyastra
20. Sikharastra
21. Vayavyastra
22. Prathanastra
23. Krauncastra
24. Hayassirastra
25. Kankalastra
26. Musalastra
27. Kapalastra
28. Kankanastra
29. Manavastra
30. Prasthapanastra
31. Prasamanastra
32. Saurastra
33. Varsanastra
34. Sosanastra
35. Santapanastra
36. Vilapanastra
37. Madanastra
38. Mohastra
39. Saumanastra
40. Samvartastra
41. Satyastra
42. Mayadharastra
43. Tejaprabhastra
44. Saumyastra
45. Sisirastra
46. Tvastastra
47. Sudamanastra

*Source: Puranic Encyclopaedia by Vettam Mani, Motilal Banarsidass(Pub.), Delhi, 2015.

ABOUT THE AUTHOR

Dr. Priyadarshi Bahinipati is an Assistant Professor and Head at the Department of History, Govt. Degree College, Longtharai Valley, Dhalai, Tripura. In his long career in academics he has obtained his M.A. and Ph.D. in History from Utkal University,Vani Vihar, Bhubaneswar, Odisha, India, M.A. in Mass Communication from Berhampur University, Bhanja Vihar, Berhampur, Odisha, India, LLB from Utkal University, Vani Vihar, Bhubaneswar, Odisha, India. He was also awarded a JRF by the ICHR, New Delhi for pursuing his research in Utkal University. He was a Research Associate in the Centre for Ambedkar Studies, Utkal University and taught History in the Post Graduate Department of History, Utkal University as a Lecturer.

The author has participated and delivered lectures in different educational institutions on several occasions. He has participated and presented a number of research papers and articles in various National and International Seminars and Conferences and also published a number of articles in National and International Journals and Books. So far, he has two published books to his credit, titled *"B.R. Ambedkar: An Enlightened Iconoclast"* and *"The Mahima Dharma: Interpreting History, Trends and Traditions"*.